INTERVIEWS WITH

❖ MUSLIM WOMEN OF PAKISTAN

[„Kovarik, Chiara Angela]

A young American woman
travels to Pakistan
and interviews Muslim women
about their lives, their hopes,
and their dreams.

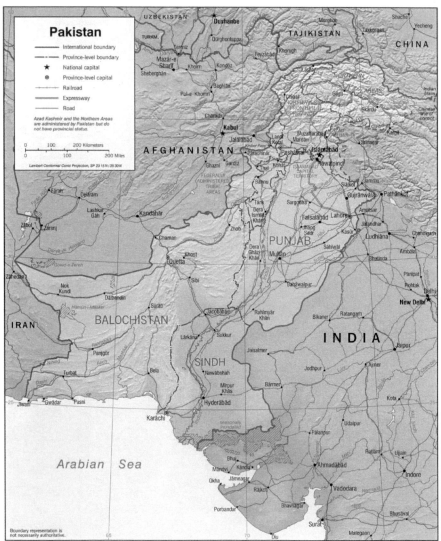

### Pakistan

— International boundary
—·— Province-level boundary
★ National capital
⊙ Province-level capital
·········· Railroad
═══ Expressway
— Road

*Azad Kashmir and the Northern Areas are administered by Pakistan but do not have provincial status.*

0   100   200 Kilometers
0   100   200 Miles

*Lambert Conformal Conic Projection, SP 23 15 N / 35 30 N*

Boundary representation is not necessarily authoritative.

Base 802863AI (C00341) 4-02

# INTERVIEWS WITH
# MUSLIM WOMEN
# OF PAKISTAN

*Chiara Angela Kovarik*

SYREN BOOK COMPANY
MINNEAPOLIS

Most Syren Books are available at special quantity discounts for bulk purchases for sales promotions, premiums, fund-raising, and educational needs. For details, write

Syren Book Company
Special Sales Department
5120 Cedar Lake Road
Minneapolis, MN 55416

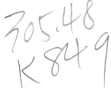

Copyright © 2005 by Chiara Angela Kovarik

Published by
Syren Book Company
5120 Cedar Lake Road
Minneapolis, MN 55416

Printed in the United States of America on acid-free paper.

ISBN-13: 978-0-929636-49-8
ISBN-10: 0-929636-49-X

LCCN 2005927228

Cover design by artist Joan Therese Kovarik.
Book design by Ann Sudmeier.

To order additional copies of this book see the form at the back of this book or go to www.itascabooks.com

*This book is dedicated to the*
## MUSLIM WOMEN OF PAKISTAN

May they retain the ancient and enriching aspects of their lives, culture, and religion that have nourished and fulfilled twenty generations before them.

May they progress forward hand in hand with us, their Western sisters and brothers, emerging as beacons of light into the shared future of our brave new world; a wondrous world of one thousand lights, but a dangerous world skirting the precipitous edge of a possible dark age of violence, preventable only by acceptance and understanding.

*We must learn to*
*live together as brothers*
*or perish together as fools.*

—Martin Luther King Jr.

*But words are things,*
*and a small drop of ink,*
*Falling like dew, upon a thought, produces*
*That which makes thousands, perhaps millions, think.*

—Lord Byron

# CONTENTS

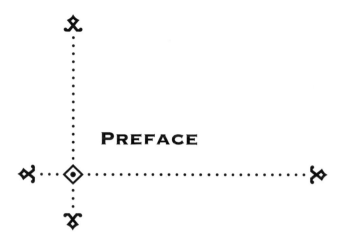

# PREFACE

IT WAS MY GOOD FORTUNE to have an
opportunity to travel to Pakistan in 2001. As I walked the
streets and alleys of ancient and great cities, such as Lahore
and Islamabad, and quaint villages such as Taxila, I began to
wonder about the women I saw and met: To what extent were
they like me? How were they different? What, indeed, was behind the veil? What could I learn from these women, cloistered
by the great walls and foreboding doors of their courtyards,
and tightly bound to their extended families?

This curiosity burned in me, so I began, shyly at first, and
with great politeness, to speak to them, to ask what they were
about. As they shopped, visited with friends and relatives, or

waited for a ride on an elaborately decorated bus or modest donkey cart, we chatted. Gradually, my questions became bolder, and my inquisitive nature overpowered my shyness and my feelings of awkwardness regarding their culture and wearing their shalwar kameez–style clothing. I began to talk to these women, and, my boldness increasing, I began to ask them questions about their daily activities, their clothes, and their families. They immediately warmed to me and conversed readily, and to my surprise they had as many questions about me as I had about them!

I was captivated, and when I returned to the United States I continued my quest. I sought out Pakistani Muslim women to continue my interviews. In addition, I remained in contact with women I had met and talked with in Pakistan. I was amazed at the trusting honesty with which they told their stories to a person they had just recently met. Their stories, though all different, for the most part contain the same basic elements. In most, there is a profound love for God and humanity, and an awe-inspiring confidence in the goodness of the world.

Behind each veil there is a story, and within each story there are universal messages. My hope is that in reading these interviews you will journey with me to Pakistan to meet these Muslim women. Join me now, as we walk down the ancient streets and alleyways of Karachi and Rawalpindi, over the sun-warmed cobblestones of great Mughal mosques, and across the soft weave of silk, hand-knotted Oriental carpets. Allow these women to open for you, as they opened for me, the doors of their courtyards and of their hearts.

## Acknowledgments

I WISH TO THANK my friend and mentor Dr. Saleem Ghani of Lahore, Pakistan, for without his help, advice, and unlimited hospitality to me during my travels, this book would not have been possible. Dr. Ghani opened many doors, allowing me to enter into the private lives and homes of Muslim women of Pakistan.

Also, I wish to thank the courageous women who consented to be interviewed, some through an interpreter, and some overcoming considerable obstacles of culture, language, and translation, who spoke openly about their fears and hopes as Muslim women in a sometimes hostile world. I could not have written this book were it not for their brave desire to share their thoughts and feelings with Western readers.

I am grateful for content and literary style suggestions from my dad and from my English teacher Mrs. Hagerty, both of whose love of the English language inspired me to pursue my dreams of writing and whose careful editing skills have made those dreams a reality.

I thank Maria Manske, Wendy Holdman, and Mary Byers of Syren Book Company, whose tireless work and expert labor turned my dream of my first book into the physical reality you now hold in your hands. These three great women of publishing turn goals into achievements to be shared by all.

I thank my mom and my dad for obtaining for me a passport when I was only six weeks old, and for taking me to twenty-two countries across our vast and infinitely amazing world. From my earliest memories, my parents have inspired in me the desire to travel the globe, to embrace other cultures, and to seek knowledge. I also am grateful to Nonna Lina, my Italian grandmother in Milan, Italy, who taught me to love learning, and to Grandma Dolores ("Dee"), who died during the writing of this book, and who sat with me for hours when I was a toddler, poring over books, their words, and their pictures. And I thank Joan Therese Kovarik, my aunt, who designed this book's stunning cover. All the photographs were taken by my mom, Maria Teresa Olivari, and me.

Finally, I wish to thank Memoona, my friend from Lahore, whose enthusiasm for this book never faltered and whose energetic zest for life is a marvel to all who meet her.

CHIARA ANGELA KOVARIK

# Interviews with Muslim Women of Pakistan

# INTRODUCTION

MANY WESTERN READERS will be surprised how difficult it was for these Pakistani Muslim women to consent to be interviewed for this book.

As an example, most of the women I approached needed first to ask permission to be interviewed from a male guardian responsible for their well-being, safety, and honor—usually the father, husband, or eldest brother. A man in that position needs to reflect upon the entire family's honor and how the interview of a female relative might affect other ongoing or future family events, such as engagements for marriage, marriageability itself, applications for citizenship or visas to travel outside Pakistan. Westerners may find this concept strange, but the extremely close bonds of extended Pakistani families, and the high importance of family reputation and personal honor in South Asia, do not permit the great degrees of personal freedom and independence of our Western lifestyle.

Some women wanted to meet with me, but the male guardian from whom they felt obliged to ask permission, denied it. None of these women disobeyed, so sadly, talking with them was not possible. Other women agreed to the interview at first, but later grew fearful and changed their minds. Some were afraid problems could arise with the U.S. government or visa-issuing authorities should they consent to the interview and its publication in a book available worldwide. Many Pakistani Muslims are mistrustful of the U.S. government after the events of September 11, 2001, and reputed heavy-handed treatment of Muslims since then. Only one woman chose to have her photograph appear in the book, and many women asked to be given a false name. The interviews with women who chose pseudonyms are indicated by an asterisk.

Many of the interviews took place completely in Urdu, the most-spoken language in Pakistan, and required one or two translators. Throughout our discussions, many women used terms that were unfamiliar to me, either because they were in Urdu or because they were associated with Islam. Definitions of these words can be found in the glossary. Most of the women checked with their Muslim Pakistani friends as to my background and reputation prior to agreeing to the interview. One woman interviewed *me* first to ensure that no ill words against Islam or against the Prophet Muhammad would appear in the book. Indeed, none has, for my intention here is not to critique an ancient religion and culture, but to convey the thoughts, hopes, and dreams of Muslim women of Pakistan.

Information in this chapter is adapted
from Amin, Willetts, and Hancock,
*Journey through Pakistan* (1997).

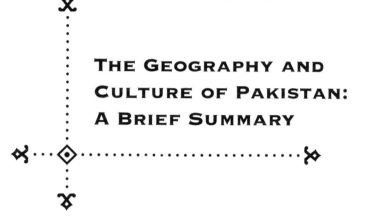

# The Geography and Culture of Pakistan: A Brief Summary

**PAKISTAN!** A historically rich region in which ancient trade routes crisscross, where Asia meets the Middle East, and modern culture is infused with the past. Established as a separate political entity only after World War II, Pakistan is a relatively new nation with a culture steeped in antiquity that is suddenly awakening to the intrusions of the twenty-first century.

Pakistan is a breathtaking country that, in some future century, could rival Italy as a destination for the world's tourists. From the beaches and coastal areas, lagoons and mangrove swamps of the South on the Arabian Sea, to the arid plateaus and sandy deserts of the West, the fertile plains of the central Indus Valley, and to the highest mountain ranges and largest glaciers on earth in the snow-covered North, Pakistan is unrivaled in natural beauty. Stretching from Islamabad to China, and reaching elevations of 28,251 feet (8,611 meters), the Karakoram Highway in the mountain passes of the North is the highest trade route in the world, and its construction is one of the greatest engineering feats in the history of Eastern or Western civilization. In fact, Pakistan's mountain passes are even higher than the summit of Mont Blanc in the European Alps, and Pakistan has more glaciers than any other region with the exception of the North and South Poles.

Bordered by Iran and Afghanistan on the west, China on the north, and India on the east, and with five hundred miles of coastline on the Arabian Sea, Pakistan, which covers 310,403 square miles (803,044 square kilometers), is a land of great diversity. Her mountainous north boasts eight of the world's ten highest peaks, including K-2, which, at 28,250 feet (8,610 meters), bows its snow-covered head in submission only to Mount Everest in the earth's doomed attempts to touch the sky. Her great bread and rice baskets are the fertile Punjab and Sind Plains, through which the Indus River flows. The rugged rocky hills and tough terrain of the mountainous North West Frontier Territories (NWFT) are considered almost a no-man's land, for the region is still ruled by warlords and tribal chiefs, as it has been for one thousand years.

Three great mountain ranges, the highest in the world, form the northern and western borders of Pakistan. These are the

Himalayas, the Karakorams, and the Hindu Kush and Sulaimans. Seven of the world's most famous mountain passes lie here, making Pakistan the gateway to Asia. Each of these passes has left its mark in the history of civilization, and the world's greatest generals and conquerors, including Genghis Khan, Tamerlane, and Alexander the Great, have led their invading armies through them. Even in recent centuries the British Empire and the Soviet Union have struggled for control of these key passes. The seven great mountain passes of Pakistan are the Khyber, the Kurram, the Tochi, the Gomal, the Bolan, the Lowari, and the Khunjrab. Even today these passes are used by the world's superpowers. The Soviet Union moved troops and supplies through them in its ten-year war in Afghanistan, as does the U.S. military and CIA in the post–September 11, 2001, U.S. wars in Afghanistan and Iraq.

Kashmir is a disputed region on the border with China, currently being contested by India and Pakistan. This region is a major tension point in the world today because both countries possess nuclear weapons. Balochistan is a rocky and less fertile region on the west, bordering Iran and Afghanistan. It has a smaller population than the other regions of Pakistan. Finally, the coastal areas on the Arabian Sea and the great city of Karachi, Pakistan's largest port, round out the amazing diversity of Pakistan.

Pakistan has four distinct seasons. The cold season extends from December to March, the hot season lasts from April to

June, the monsoon season covers the three months of July to September, and the post-monsoon season lasts from October to November.

The Islamic Republic of Pakistan's capital city, Islamabad, was designed and created in the twentieth century. President Musharraf Pervez, an army general who took control of the country and was named president on June 20, 2001, has so far been successful in balancing the pressures of Western nations such as the United States and Great Britain with the internal pressures of Islamic fundamentalists, who desire a more conservative Islamic government in Pakistan. Today, Pakistan is home to about 140 million people, and they maintain a high birthrate. Although not one of the more populous Muslim nations of the world, Pakistan is nonetheless critical for a stable international community. This role is due in part to its tensions with India in the Kashmir region and its contributions to the antiterrorism efforts of the Western powers.

Pakistan is 95 percent Muslim, and the remaining 5 percent of the population is mostly Hindu, Christian (St. Thomas the Apostle traveled to India and Pakistan, where he was martyred in the first century C.E.), and Parsi. However, of all the influences acting upon Pakistan today, Islam is the most powerful by far and serves as a unifying force for all the diverse ethnic groups. Pakistanis simply see themselves, one another, and their nation as Islamic. Islam is the focus of everything in the nation, both public and private. In fact, one of the most profound differences between Pakistani culture and the culture of the United States and Europe is that Pakistanis do not separate Islam from daily life and governance, whereas Westerners have separated religion from state.

The population is growing at the annual rate of 3 percent, which is the highest growth rate among the nine most populous countries of the world. Pakistanis strongly believe that family life, including children and grandchildren, is among the greatest gifts bestowed by Allah and provides the highest joy and fulfillment in life, incomparably more so than material or professional success.

Pakistanis are poor by Western standards, the average per capita income in U.S. dollars being $460. However, one of the Five Pillars of Islam is the giving of alms, and wherever I traveled through Pakistan, I never saw a starving person. I saw people who barely had enough to eat, but no one who appeared malnourished. Unlike many people living in India, who suffer from starvation on a daily basis, Pakistani Muslims would not tolerate the starvation of a "brother" or "sister" (as they call one another); such is their adherence to the community of Islam. More than half of all Pakistanis earn their living through fishing and agriculture, the major crops being cotton, wheat, rice, and sugarcane. Because the agrarian lifestyle is the most common one, only 39 percent of Pakistanis are literate. Urdu is the national language, and English is the official language. This latter fact is due to the British presence in India from 1612 until England was forced out of the subcontinent in 1947. When England left, it created in its wake the separate countries of India and Pakistan (which had two sections, West and East, the latter of which became Bangladesh in 1971) and tried to partition the population according to religion. Modern reminders of British colonial rule, such as the national sport, cricket, remain.

Pakistan's main exports are cotton, textiles, rice, leather items, and some of the world's most treasured handmade wool and silk carpets. Imports are industrial equipment, vehicles, iron ore, petroleum, and edible oil.

The government is parliamentary, with two houses: the Senate, with 87 senators, and a lower house with 217 members (207 are Muslim, and 10 represent minorities).

To understand Pakistan, a diverse land comprising a diverse assortment of peoples, one must understand Islam, which is a complete system that governs the beliefs and behavior of almost all Pakistanis. The Five Pillars of Islam (described in a later chapter) and the deep faith in Allah and adherence to the Koran inspire Pakistanis on a daily basis. Being a Westerner, I was surprised at the depth of belief and the ardor of the average Pakistani toward Islam. This fusing of the culture of the people with their religion is far more profound than anything we observe today in the United States or Western European nations. For example, the Western world regards private property as an absolute right. In Pakistan, however, all wealth be-

CHIARA ANGELA KOVARIK

longs to Allah, and none to human beings. In the Koran it is written, "Unto Allah belongeth whatever is in the heaven and whatsoever is in the earth." Men and women are stewards, not owners, and shall be held accountable to Allah for their stewardship, in the certain judgment that all must face after death.

In these ways, Islam influences and moderates all of Pakistani life, including social welfare programs, notions of private property, the legal system, the medical and educational systems, and the interactions of the family itself. One cannot separate Islam from Pakistan, and one cannot understand Pakistanis without understanding Islam.

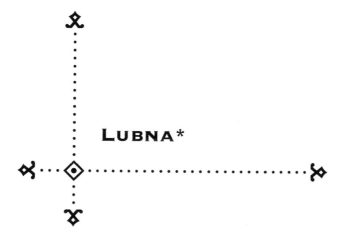

# LUBNA*

LUBNA is a small, soft-spoken older woman. Before we began the interview, she quietly excused herself to pray. In a nearby room, she softly recited prayers while kneeling on a small pale green silk handwoven carpet, facing East toward Mecca. She does this five times each day. When she finished her prayers, we began the interview. She speaks only Urdu, so her son and husband translated for us.

As they relayed my questions to her, they often forgot that Lubna, not they, was being interviewed, and they began answering the questions for her. Suddenly they would realize their mistake, laugh, and continue translating, while Lubna waited quietly. These comic scenes happened several times during our interview, and I realized these men were accustomed to speaking for her. In retrospect, I look back upon her submission during those moments when the men in her life forgot she was the interviewee and began to respond for her, and that memory more than any speaks volumes about the life Lubna has led. Clearly, patience has been a virtue well honed during her long life.

She sat on a sofa, her short, round body almost lost in her beautiful, delicately embroidered turquoise shalwar kameez. Her golden jewelry glittered in the light as she moved her hand in an occasional gesture. In the several previous times I had been with Lubna, I had never heard her speak more than five words at once, and even then shyly, so I was surprised and pleased when she opened up and answered my questions with a torrent of words which seemed out of place with this reserved, quiet woman whom I feel honored to call my friend.

Lubna was born in 1948 in Pakistan, one of six children, of whom two died. Her parents owned a small farm in the country, and, as a child, she would help them in the fields by harvesting cotton, wheat, oranges, and mangoes to sell at the village market. From a young age she enjoyed learning and eagerly sought any educational opportunities that were offered to her. The highest level of education that she could obtain in the nearby village was the equivalent of the American eighth or ninth grade. Because the nearest place offering a higher level of education was two to three hundred miles away, she was never able to continue her schooling. Nonetheless, the level of education that she achieved was uncommon among women of her generation, most of whom received little or no formal education, as they were expected to remain in the house and perform domestic and maternal duties.

In 1969, when she was twenty-one, Lubna's parents arranged a marriage between her and a young man named Abdul, whom they thought suitable for her. Lubna met Abdul only five times before their wedding day, and those meetings were chaperoned and somewhat brief. Although they both had the opportunity to refuse the marriage, they liked one another and consented to the arrangement. Their marriage has produced five children; three were born in Pakistan and two in Oman, a nearby country where Abdul relocated for work with the construction company he owned. They established a rather high standard of living among Pakistanis and were able to send all their children to the university. Now, Lubna spends most of her time running the household in Pakistan. A few times each year, she travels to the United States to visit three of her children who live and work there.

I first asked Lubna if being a Muslim woman in the modern world was in any way different from the experiences of her mother's or grandmother's generation in Pakistan. She responded resolutely. "For past generations of Muslim women," she began, "education was never a priority. Women were not expected to be educated in literary subjects, while today most women are educated. Today, women's education has been expanded to teaching women about things going on around them, such as current events. I am much more aware of what is going on in the world than my mother and grandmother were. Furthermore, my mother and grandmother gave birth to their children in their house, with only a midwife present. Now babies are delivered in hospitals, with modern equipment and doctors."

When asked what she, as a Pakistani Muslim woman, would tell the people of the United States if she could give them any message, Lubna thought for a long time before responding about family relationships. "For the people of the United States, family values must be more important. It is wrong when children leave their parents and rarely visit. In the United States, children sometimes send their parents to nursing homes when they reach old age. In Pakistan, the family will care for the elders, often welcoming them as a part of their new family. You must not forget your family! In Pakistan, family relationships are the most important bonds. Family members are always involved in one another's lives and visit their family weekly."

She paused for a while and then sighed, and I knew that she was looking through me, gazing back across time, across the decades of her life, as one might look back across the stitches in a piece of intricate embroidery over which one has painstakingly and patiently labored. Finally, she continued in a voice so soft that I could barely hear her. "As children grow older, they must seek the counsel of their elders. The elders may be able to give children insight and guidance that the child may not have come by otherwise. Becoming independent does not automatically mean one must leave one's family. It is possible to become independent while still retaining strong family bonds. Also," she added as an afterthought, "the women in the United States need to dress with appropriate modesty."

When describing the kind of world she wanted her grandchildren to be raised in, Lubna stressed the concepts of morality and ethics. "I wish for them to be raised in a world where there is no discrimination between any people," she began. She then expanded on morality, a topic that surfaced often in our interview. "Keeping strong morals and ethics is very important in our changing world. While science and technology are very important and should be used, they must take a secondary place to morality. The modern world should not compromise technology for ethics. For example, while a procedure such as abortion is technologically easy, it is not morally correct and therefore should not be done. I hope that my grandchildren will be raised in a world that expands technologically, but does not compromise morally."

When asked what it meant to her to be both a Muslim and a woman, Lubna spoke about her vital position in society. "As a

Muslim woman, I hold an important role towards all humanity. If anyone is in trouble or need, such as sickness or poverty, it is my duty to help them. Should help be required in any situation, I will willingly give it."

She added that she saw no differences between Muslim women and women of different religions. "All women are generally the same, for they all possess the same compassion towards humankind. All women worldwide have the same capabilities. Religion is separate from this basic similarity."

I asked Lubna how she thought Americans viewed Muslim women, and whether she felt misunderstood at times. She replied that she does not feel misunderstood. "I do not believe that American men think badly of me. I believe they respect me and understand that everyone around the world has their own beliefs and cultures, which must be tolerated and respected."

She continued by saying that there was no reason why Americans and Muslim women could not get along well together in today's world. I asked, "Peacefully?" to which she answered: "Americans and Muslim women can live together peacefully. If they follow and use the same beliefs and morals, they will be okay together. However, they must respect and understand each other at all times. For example, the women in the United States don't cover their bodies enough. Before Adam and Eve ate the forbidden fruit, they had light coverings over their bodies that were removed after they ate the fruit. I take this to mean that because their bodies were originally covered, and because all people come from Adam and Eve, women must dress modestly, covering their bodies. Religion will come after this modesty."

When I asked if there were any changes she would like to see in Pakistani society toward Muslim women in terms of society or jobs, Lubna responded that although things were changing, more needed to be done. "Changes are happening," she said, "but women must be equivalent to men. For example, women in Pakistan now have the right to vote. Women are given some rights, but many times those few rights are either not enforced or are trampled outright. Even though Pakistani society is supposed to be based upon Islamic law, the law is often used in favor of men. For example, if a woman must testify in a court of law, she is frequently scared into telling lies that favor men. Changes have occurred in my lifetime, but more must take place in the years to come."

Concerning her priorities in life, Lubna stated: "My first priority is my house and those who live in it. It is my duty to take care of my family. A man's priority is to provide for the family, but if for any reason he cannot, the woman must take over his responsibilities. My second priority is my children— caring for them and raising them to be good people."

At the end of our interview, I asked if the events of September 11, 2001, had changed how Lubna viewed Islam, the Western world, or the interaction between Pakistan and the

West. "Relations between Pakistan and the United States have become better since September 11, 2001," she answered. "However, I dislike the fact that when something goes wrong in relations between the Middle East and the U.S., many Americans tend to place the blame on the entire Muslim community instead of a single person. Terrorism is not a group of people in a certain country, but a group of people in the world."

My conversation with Lubna was filled with surprises. I was amazed that this shy, unassuming, extremely polite woman, whom I had met in Lahore, was brimming with inspirations just waiting to be shared, should anyone take the time to ask her opinions. I was accustomed to seeing her in my peripheral vision, taking a background role to the male members of her family and the male guests in a room, almost as if she were a quiet servant. I had never heard Lubna speak more than a few words at a time, and never on subjects other than those relating to the household, her family, or gracious hospitality offered to a guest in her home. In fact, when I originally asked her son for permission to interview her, he granted his permission but warned me that her answers would not be of any interest because she had led such a sheltered life. Little did his remarks prepare me for such depth and clarity of wisdom in Lubna's observations about life. Indeed, when I asked her each question, she took a long time to focus her exact and thoughtful response, and, when given, her responses demonstrated the depth of her beliefs on religion, the worldwide community, morality, and family. Her responses showed that she had already given these ideas much thought.

From Lubna and the other Pakistani Muslim women I was blessed with meeting and interviewing, I have realized that no matter how sheltered their lives may appear, women around the world have voices that long to be heard.

# HUMAIRA

**HUMAIRA** is a striking woman with delicate and beautiful features. She wears her sleek black hair swept behind an elaborately patterned and colorful scarf that brings out the hints of gold in her dark eyes. As we proceeded through our interview, I found myself increasingly at ease with her. She constantly smiled a slow, gentle smile, and laughed frequently and lightly. Her face was very expressive, and often I could tell what she was thinking even before she made any comment.

Humaira was born in Lahore into a Muslim family. She is one of six children, four girls and two boys. After completing high school, she worked on a bachelor's degree with majors in math and economics. She was then admitted to an M.B.A.

program, with a specialization in finance, at Punjab University in Lahore. Afterward, for three years prior to her recent marriage she worked for Bank Al Falah, which is a United Arab Emirates–based bank, formerly the BCCI (Bank of Credit and Commerce International) Bank. Humaira stresses that her religion, her parents, and her family have made a great contribution in her life. She is thankful to Allah for giving her a wonderful husband and her newborn baby daughter, and she considers both to be precious gifts to her from Allah.

My first question to Humaira concerned whether being a Muslim in the modern world was different from the experiences of her mother's or grandmother's generation in Pakistan. "Very much so," she answered. "Thirty or forty years back, the education level in Pakistan was not very high. Muslims living on the Indian subcontinent didn't have proper awareness and knowledge of Islam. The Indians who are now known as Pakistanis were greatly affected by the cultural influence of Hinduism in the Indian subcontinent. They tried to follow whatever they learned from their forefathers without questioning whether it was true or not. Even if they did have doubts, it was difficult for them to research information because there was almost no access to resources like those we have today. Now Pakistanis have convenient and prompt access to the guidance of Islam through resources such as the media and the Internet."

The media, although helpful, can also play a part in increasing animosity and causing misunderstandings between people. When I asked Humaira what she, as a Pakistani Muslim woman, would like to tell the people of the United States if she could tell them anything, she leaned forward to the edge of the silk cushions on which she sat and eagerly responded: "I would like it if not only U.S. citizens but also the rest of the Western world would not base their viewpoints about Islam or the Muslim world solely on the basis of information provided by the media. To understand and establish viewpoints, we should read other literary materials, including materials written by Muslim authors."

When asked what kind of world she wanted her children to be raised in, Humaira's response was prompt and stated with a smile: "I hope they will be raised in a modern Islamic world and have no hateful feelings towards any other religion. I dream of a world in which importance is continually given to other people's lives, property, and dignity."

When I asked her what it meant to be both a Muslim and a woman, quiet descended upon the room as Humaira thought for several minutes, after which she replied: "To me, being a Muslim woman brings more responsibilities. As part of a social structure in the Islamic world community, I, as a Muslim woman, have to take care of my family and of any domestic issues concerning my family." She had recently given birth to her first child, a daughter, and her thoughts were never far from her newborn's needs.

Her responsibilities and obligations as a Muslim woman

make her different from women of other religions. Continuing with assurance, Humaira stated: "I feel more confident being a Muslim woman. Islam gives high respect to women as being daughters, wives, and mothers. The Koran has a separate chapter titled 'Al-Nisa,' which means 'Women.' It clearly mentions the role and importance of women in daily life. Islam considers women to be the cornerstones of Islamic society. Like women of other faiths, Muslim women also share the same ideas about daily life. Some of them include striving for a better education in order to participate in the upbringing of a better family, progressing in a career that will develop a better society, and raising a well-educated family."

When I inquired about what changes Humaira would like to see in Pakistani society toward Muslim women in terms of social reform or jobs, she added, "Pakistani women should have more access to higher positions in public offices."

When I asked what her top three priorities in life were, her response was succinct. "My religion, my family, my career." I asked, "In that order?" and she immediately replied, "Yes, certainly."

Although Humaira believes that all women share the same ideas concerning daily life, she recognized that differences in thought can lead to misunderstandings. She admitted that she often feels misunderstood by Americans. Pointing to her brilliantly patterned head scarf, she continued, "If I do wear the head scarf, known as *hijaab*, Americans take me as a very conservative Muslim. However, if I don't wear it, they think I am not a true Islamic person."

In spite of multiple differences she was emphatic: "I do not see any real reason why Americans and Muslims cannot get along. The only reason would be because of incorrect images presented by the media."

Humaira declared that the events of September 11, 2001, had changed the way she viewed the interaction between Pakistan and the Western world. "My view of Islam has not changed," she began, "because my views are not affected by the heinous acts of the terrorists. However, my views on the Western world and relations between Pakistan and the Western world have changed. I now think the people of the West do not form their own views on many issues. Their views are basically dictated by the media. Right now, Pakistan is a launching pad against Afghan warlords. While Coalition operations are going on in the Indian subcontinent, as in the past, Pakistan will be considered a non-NATO ally. Therefore, I am skeptical about the Western relationship with Pakistan after the war."

When I asked her how the events of September 11 had changed the lives of Muslim women, Humaira thought for a minute before answering. "Many cultural and social issues have come up. Increased scrutiny of Muslims all over the world," she said, "has brought up these issues and created a gap that nobody, either from Muslim or non-Muslim states, is trying to bridge. For instance, a Muslim woman's head scarf is her symbol of Islam, but when a Muslim woman goes to a job interview in the United States or Europe wearing her scarf, she is denied the job because employers are afraid that they will someday be questioned by the government about hiring a Muslim woman. This is especially evident in France, under the new law banning head scarves [in schools]. To combat these issues, proper education about the Muslim faith is necessary."

Humaira acknowledged that the events of September 11 had had an impact on her personal life. She added: "It is okay to make sure that people entering the United States or European Union nations undergo background checks, but unreasonable delays due to interdepartmental problems, et cetera, for issuing visas under the label of so-called background checkups is really frustrating. For example, I am living in the United States with my husband, and my parents are living in Pakistan. Unfortunately, we cannot leave the United States and visit them in Pakistan because if we travel to Pakistan we have to apply for a [return] visa [from] there, and it takes four months for a background check as compared to people from non-Muslim states getting visas within one day. If we risk traveling to Pakistan and waiting for four months, there is the chance we will lose our jobs. In the past, U.S. immigration policy highly encouraged students, and up until December 2001, there was a high influx of immigrants to the U.S. because of its welcoming attitude towards students. In a recent survey, this influx has decreased substantially. Nonimmigrant students equally share in fields of research, and most Muslim women have the same attitude, but unfortunately, getting an F1 visa, a student visa, is extremely difficult nowadays. In most parts of the Muslim world, the educational year ends in spring. Getting a visa in time for the fall semester is very difficult, and many students end up wasting at least one year or opting to go to other countries. Given the contributions to research by foreign students and the resources in the United States, this shift will have a definite effect on the economies of both the U.S. and the world."

When I asked if she would like to make any concluding remarks, Humaira smiled and answered: "In short, Islam in no way encourages acts of terrorism. Islam even sets clear rules to be followed in the case of war. These categorically mention that in the event of war, no crops should be ruined, and no women, children, or elderly people should be hurt. Muslim nations will always deliberate before engaging themselves in any offensive action, and only heads of state, after careful deliberation with cabinet members, will engage in any such action."

My conversation with Humaira demonstrated to me the broad extent of her faith. Her beliefs are firmly rooted in Islamic scriptural tradition, and she strives to be the best mother, wife, and woman that she can be, to please both God and her community. At the same time, she is desperately trying to be understood and accepted into American society. She longs to become a part of American culture while maintaining the important and enriching aspects of her own culture. Sadly, however, during our interview Humaira described several times when she has been discriminated against or completely misinterpreted by Americans. Although these events have hurt Humaira, she notes with optimism that the way for Americans to combat these misunderstandings and prejudices is to acquire knowledge through sources other than the mainstream media. Although such situations can often be very frustrating, Humaira remains ever positive about the future for herself, her husband, and their newborn baby, and for the Americans who are now her neighbors.

## BADAR*

**BADAR** is a small, slight, older woman with beautiful, café au lait skin. She is extremely shy, and her co-workers literally had to drag her out of the back kitchen of the Pakistani restaurant in which our conversation took place. She smiled bashfully at me and seated herself on the other side of the table. Her beautifully embroidered gold and black shalwar kameez rustled as she arranged the folds modestly around her legs. Her brown eyes peered at me curiously from behind wire-rimmed glasses as I reached across to shake her slender hand. Our handshake was but a soft touch. She speaks only Urdu, so a translator was present during our interview. As the interpreter translated Badar's words, I watched her animated face and vigorous hand gestures, trying to decipher what she was saying.

Badar was born a Muslim in India, grew up in Pakistan, and spent most of her younger years as a housewife. Since 1994, she has been working in the Pakistani restaurant in which we talked. She is married and has one son, three stepchildren, nine grandchildren, and two great-grandchildren. I exclaim in shock when I hear how large her family is, for she cannot be older than sixty, and her entire face lights up in a proud smile when I tell her she has been blessed by Allah to have so large a family.

To encourage Badar to open up and tell me about her family, I first asked whether her experiences being a Muslim woman in the modern world were different in any way from the experiences of her mother's or grandmother's generation in Pakistan. She hesitated timidly while she searched for the courage to speak to me, a stranger. "Yes," she responded, smiling shyly. "My mother and grandmother were concerned mostly with domestic and homemaking duties. They were also much more conservative than the modern generation and I am. They both observed the purdah, the covering of the entire body and face, very strictly. As women, they would only leave the house if there was a very urgent need for them to do so. Nowadays, women in Pakistan can leave the house whenever they want—to go to school, to market, or to visit friends and family."

I wondered in what kind of world Badar would like her children and grandchildren to be raised. She explained: "I want my children to be raised in a modern world. They should be exposed to and know both religion and current technology. However, they should not be so totally immersed in Islam that they forget the importance of contemporary society, and vice versa. I hope they are able to find a good balance between modernity and Islam. A good balance must be forged between one's religion and one's culture.

"I would like to tell the people of the world," she continued, "that all people—from every country, culture, and religious background—can live together peacefully. This is possible if we don't define one another as Muslim or Christian or Pakistani, but simply as fellow people in the same world, all essentially the same."

When I asked Badar what it meant to her to be both a Muslim and a woman, she replied: "To me, being a Muslim woman means I believe in helping anyone, despite their religion, culture, race, or any other differences. Helping others is a Muslim woman's duty. We help with no intent of personal gain or of exploiting anyone during a difficult time. I am proud that I have such an important duty to fulfill, and I am very proud of being Muslim."

She added sincerely: "I don't see any differences, only similarities between Muslim women and women of other religions.

Women of any religion follow their faith. I follow Islam, they follow their faith. Everyone loves their religion and believes in it."

Even if no differences are evident, misunderstandings can develop, and I wondered whether Badar felt misunderstood in any way. She nodded sadly. "Before the terrorist attacks of September 11, I did not feel as though I was viewed much differently than anyone else. After the attacks, however, people often look at Muslim women with hatred. Muslims believe in loving others and in turn receiving love from them. As a Muslim woman, I am hurt and confused by this behavior. Why do people who have never met me, hate me?" Badar added that she could not find any reason why Americans and Muslims could not get along.

I then asked Badar what her top three priorities in life were. "Taking care of my family," she answered without hesitation. "It is my responsibility to make sure they are comfortable in the house and that my children are being brought up correctly. They must be raised with no hate in their hearts or in their minds. Secondly, I will take care of any poor people who need my help. I will sacrifice my comfort and well-being to help others. My third priority is to spread love amongst all people."

To conclude the interview, I asked Badar whether the events of September 11, 2001, had changed how she viewed Islam, the Western world, or interactions between Pakistan and the West. "First of all," she said, "we as a Muslim community feel as though those events were all terribly wrong. So many innocent people died. We sincerely feel their pain in our hearts. Since the attacks, some people now look at Muslims in a hateful way. It hurts me to experience these feelings. We, as a world community, should make an effort to find the good in the tragedy. We must try to work together and get along with one another in love and harmony."

I was struck by how deeply Badar cares about all people, and in particular how profoundly she cares for anyone in need, regardless of their race or creed. Throughout our interview, she stressed the importance of love among all people. She truly hopes for the best for everyone in the world, regardless of religion, nationality, or culture. She is a deep well of love, compassion, and humility, embodying what all women worldwide strive to be. She is unquestioningly empathetic toward all. However, she sometimes feels hurt when biased people do not return the love she so freely gives. She awaits with hope and patience the inevitable day when love will conquer all, and until then she does her best to live a life of love.

## RAIBA*

**RAIBA** is an outstanding woman with prominent features. Her strong nose and jaw outline the face of a
proud woman who has traveled and seen something of the
world. When she shook my hand, her grip was powerful, and
I sensed that she was a woman who knew herself well. For all
her presence, however, she was not dominating. I found myself
talking to her quite freely about many issues. As we spoke, her
black-and-gold shalwar kameez fluttered in the breeze from
a small plastic fan in the back corner of the kitchen where we
sat. The whir of the fan, the soft clink of her multiple golden
bangle bracelets, and the clanking of pots and pans provided a
comforting background melody as we spoke.

My first question to her concerned whether her experiences as a Muslim woman in the modern world were different from the experiences of her mother's and grandmother's generation in Pakistan. Raiba responded by giving comparisons not only between the generations but also between the United States and Pakistan: "Yes, there are definitely many differences. In Pakistan during my mother's and grandmother's generations, women generally operated in a sphere of domesticity. Now, they are given more educational opportunities and oftentimes work outside the home.

"Back in Pakistan," she continued, switching topics, "the women work side by side with the men, in a joint family system. Everyone helps wherever help is needed. In the United States, women have many roles in and out of the house. They maintain homemaking and domestic roles at the same time, and thus are given a lot more responsibility."

She went on: "I would encourage Pakistani women to get more involved in politics. We should raise our voices and never keep quiet about important issues. Our job is not only familial duties—we can do better than that—our job is to take part in politics. We must strive to be both homemakers and actively involved in our current world."

When I asked what kind of a world she would like her children to be raised in, Raiba responded: "A world in which there is no violence, prejudice, or racism. A peaceful world in which there lingers no trace of hatred towards anyone."

Concerning her thoughts on being both a Muslim and a woman, she proudly declared: "I have always been and always will be proud to be both a Muslim and a woman. I have never felt bad regarding either." She promptly added that as a Muslim woman, she did not consider herself different from women of other religions. There was no hesitation in her voice.

I then asked Raiba how she thought Americans viewed Muslim women and whether she felt in any way misunderstood. "Yes," she replied after a moment of thought. "Americans sometimes think Muslim women don't have rights equal to those of men. However," she declared, leaning forward eagerly in her seat, her voice booming now as she became visibly excited, "that belief is very untrue! Islam *does* give women equal rights as men. In fact, it is the only religion that gives women the right to divorce. Women have the right to work side by side with men, the right to share their money, and also the right to keep their money if they wish to do so. They are in no way obligated to give any of the money they earn to their husband or anyone else. Although Islamic society is still male-dominated, women *do* have rights.

"Muslim women often feel misunderstood in this aspect. Muslim society must change somewhat. It needs to become more liberal. There should be a much greater emphasis placed on education for women. Pakistani women should all try hard to get a good education so that they can work, build up a steady income to care for their family, and decrease poverty levels in

Pakistan. Pakistani society must change in its views towards women—women must be given the opportunity to leave the house and enter the workforce."

When asked what her top priority was, Raiba answered: "My children are my top priority. My main concern is giving them a good education and raising them to be good citizens."

I wondered whether the events of September 11, 2001, had changed how Raiba viewed Islam, the Western world, or the interactions between Pakistan and the Western world, so I asked her to discuss this issue. "There have been both good and bad effects of September 11 on the Muslim community," she began. "A bad outcome is that many Muslims are now judged negatively by the world just because they are Muslim. However, there have been a surprising number of good outcomes. For one, since the attacks, people of the world have become less ignorant about Islam. Because the media are largely biased and one-sided, people are seeking information about Islam and the Muslim world through other sources. This curiosity leads them to reading and research, and through this, people are able to compare what they discover about the Muslim world with what they are being told by the largely biased media. Since September 11, there has been a greater discussion of these topics amongst people, and awareness is growing. The best-selling book in the world is now the Koran: it now outsells the Bible. The Koran has never changed in the history of Islam. Islam is now both the world's largest and fastest-growing religion. Many people are converting every day, meaning there must be something in the Islamic religion that makes people fundamentally change. I am very happy that the world today suddenly has an increased interest in Islam."

Raiba is a strong, determined woman of powerful presence and forceful thoughts. From our interview I realized the depth of her pride in her religion. She burns with a passion to teach others about the wonders of Islam and to spread her own love for Islam worldwide. Her clearly stated and well-defined thoughts show that she embraces all aspects of being a Muslim woman, and at the same time, she notes changes that need to occur in Pakistani society as her beloved country struggles to emerge into the modern era. She is very forward-thinking and encouraging toward all Pakistani women who wish to make changes in society. She demonstrates that a modern Muslim woman can be intensely committed to her religion and lifestyle, and at the same time recognize areas where improvements and modernizations are needed and eagerly work toward a better future for all Pakistanis, both men and women.

# MEHMOODA

MEHMOODA is a short, curvy woman with wavy black hair pulled back into a loose ponytail. She is wearing bright-red lipstick and a matching hand-knitted sweater, which she shyly smoothes as she seats herself across the table from me. She is a very happy woman; her face is constantly breaking into a beautiful smile as we chat.

Mehmooda left Pakistan at an early age to attend school in Saudi Arabia before moving to the United States and marrying. She has a beautiful two-year-old son, and she beams with pride when she mentions him. She works two jobs to help support her family, at a Pakistani restaurant and at a large food-processing company. Dark circles under her eternally cheery eyes are evidence of tiredness.

When I heard that she had lived in Saudi Arabia for many years, I asked Mehmooda if she had been to Mecca and had completed the Hajj, the pilgrimage to Mecca, which is one of the Five Pillars of Islam. She immediately lit up, a large smile brightening her face. "Oh, yes!" she exclaimed, barely able to contain her excitement. "I went a few years ago. As a woman, I wore a black shalwar kameez and a veil, and I was not allowed to wear makeup. All are equal in the Hajj. The men all wear seamless two-piece white garments. The reason all the men and women wear the same thing is to discourage any judgments based upon appearance. This equality in dress symbolizes the equality of all people before Allah. It was so beautiful inside! I was enveloped by the most striking feeling of peace I have ever felt. There are no words to describe the experience of the Hajj."

I then asked Mehmooda if, being a Muslim woman, her experiences were in any way different from those of her grandmother's generation in Pakistan. "Oh, yes," she said, opening up more as she and I became more comfortable with one another. "There are many big and noticeable differences between the generations. For one, women never used to leave the house. The house was their area—the outside was not. My dad never let my mom work, but I now work and help to support my family."

When I asked her what kind of world she would like her children to be raised in, Mehmooda smiled shyly and replied: "A peaceful world. Right now the world is rapidly changing. It is turning into a place where many bad things happen. I hope an end will be put to these evil ways. I want my children to always be safe, and never fearful of anything."

She told me that she was very proud to be both a Muslim and a woman. When I asked whether anything made her different from women of other religions, she replied, "No," and after a moment of thought, she added, "Everyone in every religion has their differences, but they depend upon the person, not the religion." She continued: "I feel somewhat misunderstood by Americans when they assume that I am different because I am Muslim. I wish they could realize, like I have come to realize, that Americans and all Muslims, men and women, can get along very well in our world."

When I asked Mehmooda if there are any changes she would like to see in Pakistani society in terms of social reform or jobs, she brightened immediately, and I realized she had already given this idea much thought. "Yes!" she responded enthusiastically. "In Pakistan, women don't work like they do over in the United States. In Pakistan, if women work, they are looked down upon and made to feel inferior or bad in some way." She sighed and continued: "But change won't be simple. It is so much easier said than done. It will definitely take more than one generation. One way that it can come about more quickly," she added, "is to expand educational opportunities for women in Pakistan. By doing so, women will become more broad-minded and forward-thinking."

I then asked her what her top three priorities in life were. She responded with a smile. "My baby, my husband, and my family. In addition, it is very important to me to always maintain the respect of my entire family, including my extended family. The extended family is so important to Pakistanis. That is a difference between life in Pakistan and life in the U.S. Pakistanis are very close to their families, and maintaining respectability of the whole family is very important."

My interview with Mehmooda, although short, was powerful and enlightening. She described with feeling her hopes and dreams for a better world for herself and her children. She expressed contentment with the present and hope for the future.

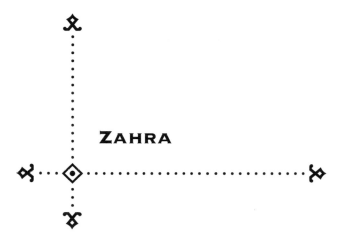

## ZAHRA

ZAHRA was born in Pakistan and went to Pakistan's University of Engineering and Technology in Lahore. After graduation, she worked as a teaching assistant at Lahore University of Management Sciences (LUMS), one of the most prestigious academic institutions in Pakistan. She later went on to receive a master's degree from LUMS. She lives in Pakistan and currently is working as a researcher in the Optimization Department in a telecommunications company called Mobilink, a subsidiary of Orascom Telecom. Mobilink is the largest telephone operator in Pakistan and holds 60 percent of the subscriber base in Pakistan.

Zahra has three sisters. One, a doctor who is a year older

than she, is married and has a beautiful one-year-old baby boy who is the joy of her life. One of Zahra's younger sisters is at the University of Engineering and Technology studying chemical engineering, and her third sister will take her Level O exams in May 2005. Zahra's mother has a master's degree in physics and has been teaching for thirty years. Her father is a former judge who continued to practice law after his retirement until his recent death.

Zahra describes her family as semiconservative people with strong values, and she eagerly tells stories of how her siblings strive to remain close wherever they may find themselves, and try to stick together through both the joyous and the sorrowful moments of their lives. This is a degree of intense closeness and sibling intimacy that many Westerners like myself are unlikely ever to experience.

When Zahra told me stories about her family, I wondered if she thought being a Muslim woman in modern Pakistan was different from the experiences of her mother's or grandmother's generations. "I believe things have changed greatly over the years," she began thoughtfully. "My grandmother and mother both worked, but the nature of our jobs is different, which is in itself an indication of the way things are progressing. Both my mother and grandmother taught in an all-girls school, while I work as an engineer in a department where I am the only female. My family does not have an issue with that. So this is itself a measure of change."

As a Pakistani woman, Zahra told me she found it strange that family ties in the United States are not very strong. "The ease with which people walk out on marriages and walk out on their parents once they can support themselves," she continued, "is quite disturbing to me as a Pakistani. Because we are all humans, I believe our nature cannot be that different, and it leads me to wonder: If people in Pakistan can survive twenty-five or more years in marriage, why cannot the same be true for people in the U.S.? I believe it is just a matter of patience."

I asked Zahra in what kind of world she would like her children to be raised. Her response was prompt: "I believe my parents have struggled and sacrificed to give me the best of everything—ample food, good clothing, and a quality education. Therefore, I would primarily want my children to be raised in a similar environment. May I do for them what my parents have done for me."

When I asked what it meant to her to be both a Muslim and a woman, Zahra replied: "Being a Muslim is one thing that I would never want to lose. We belong to a family of Syeds (descendants of Our Holy Prophet, Peace Be upon Him), and the way religion has been instilled in me is something I would never give up. I believe that I could not personally be close to God if I were not a Muslim.

"As for being a woman," she continued, "sometimes, living in Pakistan, I think our activities are hampered because a lot of gender bias still exists. I feel that some tasks would become much easier if I belonged to the opposite sex. However, there are advantages to being a woman as well. Women are given distinguished and good treatment compared to men in Pakistan. For example, if my car broke down, and that of a male colleague also broke down at the same time, at least a dozen people would come to help me, while the response to the male colleague would be different. Most of the men in Pakistan believe women to be weak creatures and consider it their duty to protect them."

As a Muslim woman, Zahra acknowledged several differences between her and women of other religions: "The first and foremost thing is that I pray to Allah five times a day. The second would be the moral constraints that our religion places upon women. For example, any extramarital relationships are considered illegal and punishable by our Islamic law. Though we, as Muslims, do not strictly follow all the things our religion asks us, we try to conform as much as possible. This is helpful in building a good and strong character as well as making ourselves into good human beings. The basic idea in this regard is that Islam teaches men and women restraint, self-control, so as to distinguish humankind from other species."

When I asked how she believed Americans viewed Muslim women and if she felt misunderstood, Zahra admitted that she had not had much exposure to the American people, and therefore any opinion she would express would be based solely upon assumption. However, she added that she did not see any reason why Americans and Muslim women could not get along well. "It depends upon the kind of interaction," she said. "If I were living in America, I would try to get along with the American women by considering them first as human beings."

When asked if there were any changes she would like to see in Pakistani society in terms of social reform or jobs, Zahra answered: "I think the way Pakistani society is progressing in terms of jobs for women is very healthy and optimistic. As I stated earlier, I am the only female engineer in the Optimization Department at my company. Since people are becoming aware that for women to contribute successfully to society they must be educated, a lot of openings have recently been created for women in all kinds of jobs."

I then asked Zahra to list her top three priorities in life. "My first and foremost priority in life," she began, "is my duty to Allah. It is my obligation to please him by doing good to others and by being honest and truthful. My second most important priority is my duty to my only living parent—my mother. Since I have lost one parent, it would be unacceptable for me to lose the other. I try within all my means to help my mother as much as I can and support her, even though my job is very demanding and often requires me to work twelve hours a day. My third highest priority in life is my career. I want to be monetarily secure so I am able to support my family and all who need my help, while still managing to move up the ladder of success. I am quite ambitious. Also equally important would be having a good life partner, as one cannot spend their entire life alone. God has made man a social animal and not an isolated one."

Finally, I asked Zahra if the events of September 11, 2001, had changed how she viewed Islam, the Western world, or interactions between Pakistan and the Western world. "I think Western society has taken a biased and negative attitude towards the Muslim world," she stated firmly. "Westerners are being vindictive to quite an extent. I strongly believe in fairness towards all, irrespective of caste, creed, or religion."

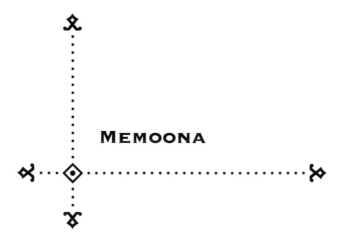

## MEMOONA

I FIRST MET MEMOONA at her family's home in Lahore, Pakistan, and even though we were reared on continents half a world apart, she in the Eastern Muslim tradition and I in the Western Christian tradition, and even though a chasm of experiences separated us, we discovered that we have many similarities and we were destined to become close friends.

Memoona was born in Muscat, Oman, but is a native Pakistani because almost all of her life has been spent in that country. She is twenty-seven years old. She received a degree in electrical engineering in Pakistan and then pursued her master's degree in the United States at the University of St. Thomas in

St. Paul, Minnesota. She now works as a software developer and consultant specializing in database construction and management and data transformations, which is considered a "hot" area of expertise in modern information technology.

Memoona recognized that being a Muslim woman in the modern world is different from the experiences of her mother's or grandmother's generation in Pakistan. She began by observing: "Today in modern society, women have more resources to learn about our own religion. We can read and listen to the scholars who have worked so hard to do research on not only Islam but other religions as well. Today, we can differentiate between the actual teachings of Islam and the myths people have been following. Most of the Muslim women in my mother's and especially my grandmother's time followed a lot of practices which were not even truly Islamic. The reason was not that they were trying to change the religion but their lack of education. These women followed what was told to them. They didn't have many resources to find out the exact meanings of all the teachings. Whatever was told to one generation was followed and passed on to the next generation."

To clarify, Memoona offered a couple of examples: "Some women used to go to the shrines of very famous Sufis. It is okay to go to mosques associated with these shrines, since a mosque is a place of prayer. It is also okay to pray for those people who have worked hard and spent a lot of time explaining the meaning of the religions. But the problem starts when people start going to these shrines and asking from these Sufis in their prayers. In Islam, there is a direct relationship with Allah. There is no middleman. We should pray, 'Allah! Please give me my wish.' We should not go to shrines and pray, 'Sufi! Please give me my wish.' These kinds of practices imply that people are not believing in God, but indirectly thinking that the Sufis or religious leaders are the source of fulfilling their prayers, which is incorrect. Allah listens to our prayers directly. We may pray for one another, but neither Allah nor the Sufis ask people to pray in this manner.

"Another misconception held by many in the past generations of women in Pakistan," she continued, "was that if girls go to school, they will become bad. Furthermore, this conception was somehow linked to Islam, which was extremely wrong, because Islam itself emphasizes female education. The women in Islam are allowed to be educated and present their points of view to other people, especially family members."

Memoona went on: "There is one very cruel and wrong practice which I think might still prevail in the Sindh province of Pakistan. It used to exist in remote villages when I was a child. If a girl did not get a suitable candidate for marriage, the men of the family might force her to 'marry the Koran.' This is *totally wrong* and is not Islamic at all, but these women and many other people were made to believe that it was religious. Lack of education made them believe it. The reason some families made their girls take part in this act was because they did not want their family money and property to go out of their families. However, there is nothing Islamic in this act. These women need a lot of help because they cannot go anywhere and they are probably guarded by violent men."

I did not understand Memoona's phrase "marry the Koran," so I asked her to elaborate. I was surprised and saddened by her explanation: "I mentioned this piece of information as a difference between women of this world and the old times. The misconception and mistreatment mentioned above were in earlier days in the province of Sindh in Pakistan. The men of those tribes did not want their business and money to go out of their families, so they created a wrongful custom by themselves. They declared that their daughters should be 'married to the Koran' if they did not find suitable marriage candidates within their extended families. These women were forbidden to marry any man outside of the extended family. A woman who was forced to marry the Koran could not marry and was made to stay at home and read the Koran for the rest of her life, along with performing the other household chores. These men claimed this tradition was Islamic, which it is not, and in fact this tradition does not even make sense in Islam. This is non-Islamic and has nothing to do with Islam at all, but people in the Sindh region of Pakistan used to think this was religious.

"These are the kind of things which some Pakistani Muslim women believed to be part of Islam," Memoona concluded.

"Today, in this modern world, we have more resources and the ability to find exact details about Islam. We know that we have got to ask Allah directly for our needs. Today I know that education is not going to spoil me. I know that Islam does not stop me from giving my point of view to anyone in my family. I can learn Sharia and find the details of my religion. And there are many other aspects as well where education in today's world has helped a lot of Muslim women understand religion in its true meaning."

I marveled at the great reverence all the Pakistani Muslim women I interviewed paid to Muhammad, so I asked Memoona, "Muhammad was illiterate, is that correct?" She took no offense at my question and casually responded, "The Prophet Muhammad was illiterate, but Allah cleansed his heart and made it open for education before sending the Koran to him. Muhammad, Peace Be Upon Him, dictated the Koran to people who could read and write. Those faithful companions wrote down the verses as they came to the Prophet." Muslims believe it was the Archangel Gabriel who dictated the Koran to Muhammad, and this is the same Archangel Gabriel who in Christian tradition appeared to the Jewish virgin Mary announcing the incarnation of Jesus.

I next asked Memoona what she, as a Pakistani Muslim woman would tell the people of the United States if she could tell them anything. "I would like the people of the United States, as well as the rest of the world, to know a few things," she began. "First of all, please don't assume anything about Islam. One must read the teachings of Islam and the Koran to understand what Islam really means. Islam is an extension of all the monotheist religions. It is an extension of Judaism and Christianity. Just looking at a few people does not represent the whole Muslim community.

"Secondly, there is something that is very important for the people of the United States to understand. Islam is a religion of love, chastity, and discipline. We as Muslim women cover our heads because that is a part of our religion. These are not rules made by men. They are not rules which have been taken into the hands of men and misused. Furthermore, covering our heads and bodies does not mean that Muslim women are conservative or backward.

"In addition, we worship and offer prayers as instructed in our religion. For Muslims, praying is a way of gratefulness and love towards Allah. These are the things which have been taught to the Apostle and passed from generation to generation.

"One thing which is really important to understand is the difference between Islam and the culture of a country. There are several cultural aspects in a country which should not be given the name 'religion,' and in our case should not be termed 'Islamic.' This has always caused misconceptions among people who are not native to Pakistan and have relatively little knowledge about Islam. I'll give a simple example. Weddings, as we know them, are important aspects of human life. In Islam there are certain rules and rituals which need to be performed in order for a matrimonial relationship to be authentic. Once—and if—these requirements are fulfilled, the marriage between a man and a woman is done. In Islam, these requirements are as follows: Number one is Nikah. This is the Islamic way of binding a man and a woman together in matrimony. The man and the woman are asked in front of witnesses if they accept this bond. If they do, then several verses are read from the Koran. At the end, people pray for the couple. Secondly, before finalizing the Nikah, there is a certain monetary amount set for the bride from a member of the groom's family. The purpose of this money is to make certain the girl will have enough money to start a life *if* the couple cannot get along well and must go through the process of divorce. This again leads into complicated details, but now let's keep in mind that this is one of the ritual steps of an Islamic wedding. Thirdly, the groom gives a feast to his family and the bride's family. The wedding is declared final if the above three requirements are fulfilled. Now people have added several other traditions to the weddings according to where they live. Some people arrange for several days of feasting surrounding the wedding day. Others wear certain kinds of clothes. However, these things are not representative of Islam, but of the culture of a country."

When I asked Memoona what kind of world she wants her children to be raised in, she answered: "One thing is for sure—we want our children to learn about Islam. It is important because the Koran not only talks about Islam and the rules and regulations taught by the Prophet Muhammad but also speaks of other past religions. The kids should know what was revealed as part of their religion. We want our kids to learn and understand the teachings of Islam and the purpose of the religion. We want them to understand that Islam is not just a name or some kind of cult—it is a religion and a way of life. Also," she continued, "we want them to learn and explore the resources in this world. They can be very good Muslims along with being very good engineers, doctors, businessmen, or any professional who needs talent. They must understand that Islam does not stop people from learning and benefiting from the infinite sources Allah has spread around them."

Memoona was very excited when asked what it meant to her to be both a Muslim and a woman. "That's a very interesting question!" she replied. "When I look at myself as a woman, I always see myself not only as a woman but as a Muslim woman. Islam has given a definite and respectable place to women in the world and in their family circles. As a woman, I know that I am a basic part of a family system. The household is dependent upon me. I can help my family financially if needed. I am responsible for taking care of my husband and children, and so is my significant other. These are the same things that I have learned being a Muslim. As a woman, I know I should be taken as a respectable human being, not a piece of amusement or entertainment for others. These are the same things that Islam has taught its followers.

"As a woman," she said, waxing even more animated, "I am aware that if I am married, then I have to abide by the matrimonial laws. I must be loyal to my husband, and my husband to me, and protect my family from any wrongdoings. I have learned these same lessons from Islam. Furthermore, when I leave my home for any reason such as work or school, I am taking the responsibility of representing myself, my family, and everything that belongs to me, to the outside world. I must make certain that I do not do anything which is either religiously or ethically wrong. Islam is a religion which does not teach you to dictate to others. It says that one must first correct himself or herself before teaching others. I believe this is an important lesson for all. In addition, there is no rule in Islam which states that women cannot educate themselves in the world. And that is what I deserve, if I simply take myself as a woman and keep religion aside, while still remaining mindful of my values."

To expand upon the question of women and religious values, I asked Memoona if, as a Muslim woman, she thought anything made her different from women of other religions. She responded thoughtfully: "The only way in which I feel different from women of other faiths—be they Catholics, Jews, or any other religion—is the differences in their faith and the way they worship. All women practice their religion as they have learned and explored. I have met a lot of Christian women, Jewish women, and women of other faiths. All of them try to practice their religion and bring up their children according to ethics and the rules and regulations set out by God. To me, they are all respectable."

I next asked Memoona how she, as a Pakistani Muslim woman, thought Americans viewed Muslim women and if she felt misunderstood. "My experience shows," she began eagerly, "that American people think Muslim women wear the hijaab because they are forced to do so, and that it has nothing to do with the Islamic religion. Covering one's body is part of Islam, and it should be implemented in Muslim families. The problem arises when people try to take matters into their hands to a great extent and end up forgetting the actual ways the rules are to be implemented. This is where misconceptions come into existence. Muslim women can sometimes be suppressed by men, but this suppression is committed by specific men or families due to their nature as human beings; suppression does *not* stem from the Islamic religion. Islam does not suppress women: It is some men and some families which suppress some women.

"Also, people think that Muslim women do not enjoy life fully since they are covered most of the time and pray every day. That is most definitely not true! We enjoy our lives as much as anyone else. The teachings of Islam have opened our minds and our hearts, and we are able to love more fully each and every moment of our lives. However," she added sadly, her voice softly falling as she filled with emotion and her eyes welled with near-tears, "this is true as far as my life goes, but there are women out in the world who have been deprived of the joy of education and life under the false name of Islam. When these poor women are made to do things under the name of Islam which are not really Islamic, they find it hard to love other human beings and even their own religion because they are never given a chance to learn the straight facts. This happens in Muslim countries where girls are not allowed to be educated or to express their point of view in front of their families."

Memoona sighed and looked over my shoulder, out onto a field, where poor farmers were hand-harvesting vegetables and loading them unto a donkey cart under an intense sun, and I knew my friend was lost in thoughts about places in Pakistan she has been, Pakistani families she has known. As she struggled to find adequate words to convey these concepts to me, a Western woman, I realized that although we were similar in many ways, a chasm of experiences separated us.

Misconceptions can greatly affect relationships, and I was curious whether they had in any way affected Memoona's, so I asked her if she saw any reason why American and Muslim women could not get along famously together. She responded: "I believe you mean American non-Muslim women. This is more an issue of human interaction than of religion. I don't see any reason why American and Muslim women cannot get along well. If both sides respect the other, they can live in harmony. Tolerance is the virtue which can keep any two human beings together even if they have entirely opposite views. Furthermore, if anyone says that Muslim women cannot live with or tolerate anything having to do with non-Muslim women because it not allowed in Islam, they are wrong. It is clearly stated in the Koran that Muslims not only should accept that other religions exist in the world, but also that Muslims should respect people of other religions and tolerate their different points of view."

I asked Memoona if there were any changes she would like to see in Pakistani society in terms of social reform or jobs. She replied: "Pakistani society has started changing in several ways. People are emphasizing education in order to make themselves useful in the modern world and in their religion. Today, women receive much more respect than they did in past generations. If I could do something, I would like people to learn the actual meaning of Islam. It is not only the outside world that has wrong ideas about Islam. There are Muslim people living in Pakistan who don't know a lot of things about the true meaning of Islam. We are not all perfect in our knowledge. We have to learn from each other and then teach our knowledge to others. We must share the knowledge we are taught from our struggles."

In spite of change, priorities often persist. When I asked

Memoona what her priorities in life were, she answered: "I am in a phase where I am learning about Islam and other religions as well. I want to be a person who strongly holds on to Allah's religion and follows his teachings. At the same time, I want to keep myself abreast of worldly knowledge and upcoming technologies." She was eager and moved to the edge of the sofa, her voice rising in excitement as she explained: "I want to use my efforts and knowledge to shape up my family. If I learn something useful, I would like my family to know it as well. However, I don't want to be the source of any information being taught incorrectly. If I am with them, I wish that we are able to not only educate ourselves, but to enjoy life as well."

Finally, I asked Memoona if the events of September 11, 2001, had changed the way she viewed Islam, the Western world, or the interaction between Pakistan and the Western world. She responded: "The events of September 11, 2001, have made me search for a lot of answers in the Islamic religion. My view of Islam has become even clearer than it was before. Conditions in both the Muslim world and the Western world have become tense. Groups have developed who really hate Muslims because they think Islam and all Muslims are the cause of such terrorist attacks. These types of groups believe all Muslims think the same way, which is untrue. But at the same time, groups in the Western world have formed who are open to finding the truth. Muslim countries including Pakistan are trying hard to get along with Western countries. Muslim countries are striving to tell Western countries that they are not terrorists and they are not helping terrorists."

Throughout my conversation with Memoona, I was amazed at the clarity with which she answered each question. She took each question to heart and answered it thoughtfully, oftentimes giving examples to elucidate. Her thoughts show that she is deeply and passionately interested in spreading knowledge of Islam to the world. Through this, she hopes to settle any misunderstandings about Islam, Muslims, or Muslim women from Pakistan, and to be a positive agent for change in a world heading toward divisiveness.

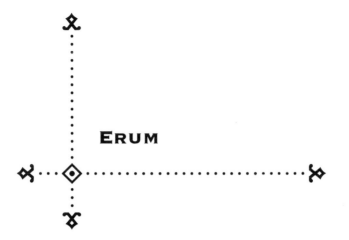

# ERUM

ERUM was born in Lahore, Pakistan, into a Muslim family of the Kashmiri caste (the name refers to people who are from Kashmir but no longer live in that region, or to their descendants). She is one of five children—four girls and a boy. After learning Koranic recitations at a young age, she was sent to school. Following graduation, she went to college and earned a degree in economics and statistics. She then completed a master's degree in finance at the University of Punjab and worked in two freight forwarding companies for three years. After she married her husband, Rashid, she moved from Pakistan to Canada.

We began our interview by discussing whether Erum's experiences as a Muslim woman in the modern world had been in any way different from the experiences of her mother's or grandmother's generation in Pakistan. "Yes," she replied enthusiastically, "today's world is much more advanced in every field, and science has proved many facts which Islam had revealed fourteen hundred years ago. Also, in today's world, Muslims are much more broad-minded than they were in the past. Muslims used to be a great deal more conventional. Now we are more proud of our religion because its facts and prophecies have been proved true and continue to be proved true every day."

I asked Erum what she, as a Pakistani Muslim woman would tell the people of the United States if she could tell them anything. She paused to reflect and then responded thoughtfully: "Pakistan is a country of Muslims living in peace. Some terrorists have made us notorious for being Muslims, but otherwise, all the Muslims in Pakistan live in peace, love, and harmony with one another. We Pakistanis take care of our neighbors, relatives, and poor and disadvantaged people in times of need. Pakistanis are, in general, innocent poor people. We live together peacefully and never hesitate to help anyone who requires need, even if we do not know him or her.

She carefully smoothed the folds of her shalwar kameez as it cascaded gracefully across her lap in a soft falling of silk, choosing her words as precisely as she chose the exact placement of each fold of her garment. She did not hurry in her response, such was her precision. "A Muslim woman," she continued, "is caring, loving, and faithful to her husband, father, and brothers. She spends her life taking care of her siblings and family while growing up, and once married additionally cares for her children and her husband's family, even if they do not get along very well. She remains faithful all her life. She raises her children in her love and care and is very ambitious. She lives happily without the luxuries of life because of the contentment taught to her by mothers of believers."

To expand upon Erum's thoughts regarding family and children, I asked her about the kind of world in which she would like her children to grow up. "I want my children to be raised in a pure Islamic atmosphere," she began, "where girls use hijaab and are shy and modest. A world in which they are well liked, not only by members of their religion, but by the whole world. It is also important to me that they be able to easily understand the concepts of the Holy Prophet, Peace Be Upon Him."

When I asked Erum what it meant to her to be both a Muslim and a woman, her reply was prompt. "It means everything to me!" she began with excitement. "I believe that Islam has given maximum rights to women. It has given them equal rights in inheritance, in education, and in all basic needs and aspects of life, which no other religion has. Before Islam came about as a religion, some people used to bury their daughters alive in graves! For this, and for so many other reasons, I believe I am the luckiest person on earth to be a Muslim woman!"

Continuing on the topic of being a Muslim woman, I asked Erum what, if anything, made her, as a Pakistani Muslim woman, different from women of other religions. She responded: "Islam has given women great respect. It asks women to cover themselves completely to protect themselves from the bad intentions of others. It gives mothers three times more respect than it does fathers, and those who look after their mother are promised *Jannah* paradise. In addition, it gives husbands the responsibility of looking out for their wives' well-being and caring for them."

I did not understand the term "Jannah paradise," so I asked Erum to define this expression. She replied, "Jannah is paradise or heaven, which is a promised place for people who have done good deeds in their lives. Jannah is an Arabic word for 'paradise' or 'heaven.'"

Erum expressed her opinion about misunderstandings because this topic was very much on her mind and often surfaced in our conversations: "Americans think Muslim women are outdated and orthodox due to the fact that we cover ourselves. They believe that Islam is imposing restrictions on us. First of all, these are not restrictions! Secondly, if they see these rules as restrictions, then they are restrictions made only for our benefit, and are not harmful to us in any way."

To clarify her thought, I asked Erum if any of the misunderstandings that she listed could lead to Americans and Muslim women not getting along. "Yes," she responded firmly.

"Americans and Muslim women cannot get along because they have differences in their practices of life. Muslim women wear different clothes than American women, eat different foods, and live their sex life differently. They have totally different lifestyles, so how *can* they get along with one another?"

When I asked Erum if there were any changes she would like to see in Pakistani society toward women in terms of social reform or jobs, she responded: "Yes. I would like there to be more respect towards women in accord with Islam, and more acknowledgment of women's efforts both inside and outside the home. They should have more sexual protection and they should be given jobs according to their qualifications and not anything else. They should be given due respect and positions which match their qualifications. They should be given more confidence!"

I switched topics by asking Erum to describe her priorities in life, to which she replied without hesitation: "My number one priority is living my life according to the teachings of Islam and Sunnah, and the path of the beloved Prophet, Peace Be Upon Him. Secondly, I want to train my children according to the guidelines of my religion. Thirdly, I want to achieve something good for the whole *Umma* before I die."

Near the end of our conversation, I asked Erum whether the events of September 11, 2001, had changed the way she viewed Islam, the Western world, or the interaction between Pakistan and the Western world. She responded: "The events have not in any way changed my views of Islam! They were actions taken by a group of Muslims, not the entire Islamic religion. I do not judge Islam by certain Muslims' actions, because if we do so then we cannot go to Christians because they too are not acting upon their own religious teachings.

I asked Erum how she felt the Western world viewed Pakistani Muslims in particular, and Muslims in general, after the events of September 11, 2001, and in light of the ongoing terrorist manhunts across the rugged and almost inaccessible terrain of the mountainous Pakistan–Afghanisan border. She replied: "Concerning the Western world, I have come to know that Westerners are very biased against Muslims and have made the lives of all Muslims difficult after the events of September 11. As for the interaction between Pakistan and the Western world, it was not a relationship characterized by freedom in the first place. After the terrorist attacks, Pakistan has come under a lot of pressure from people in the Western world. Leaders use their power to pressure us Pakistanis, and being a poor country, we Pakistanis are unable to make our own decisions and take our own actions."

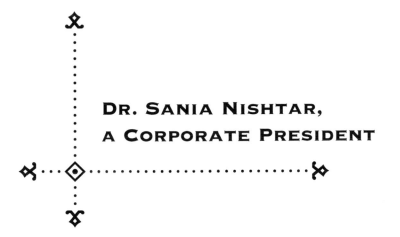

## Dr. Sania Nishtar, a Corporate President

**I MET DR. SANIA NISHTAR** at an international conference on women's health in Orlando, Florida. I was struck by her powerful presence immediately when she walked into the room. Her vibrantly colored shalwar kameez was softly flowing in the gentle breeze of her dramatic entrance, and everyone in the room looked toward her, regardless of the meetings that were under way. Dr. Nishtar has presence. She is a striking and beautiful woman, and her clothes, although appropriately modest in Muslim tradition, are exceptional in their colors, beauty, and style. Upon seeing her, one is disabused forever of the notion that Muslim women in traditional dress cannot be elegantly and fashionably attired.

Sania is the founder and president of Heartfile Corporation, a published author, and an inventor. She travels around the world giving talks on the topic of her passionate desire, the strengthening of public health care systems in the developing world, especially innovative resource-sensitive approaches for the prevention and control of noncommunicable diseases. She is a member of the Royal College of Physicians and has a Ph.D. in health sciences.

Sania's academic career combines a clinical background in cardiovascular medicine with a wide public health and policy perspective. Her work in the health sector is focused on influencing health policies at the global level and reorienting them to the changing health dimensions in the wake of the worldwide epidemiological transition in health, which is especially acute and visible in the developing world. Her goal is to strengthen the public health planning and delivery systems in the developing countries.

This focus is reflected in her brainchild and work with Heartfile, a nonprofit public health company she founded in Pakistan in 1999 with her own resources. Within six years she has developed Heartfile into a leading health sector force that works in collaboration with the Pakistan Ministry of Health, the government of Pakistan, and the World Health Organization (WHO).

As chair of the Foundations Advisory Board of the World

Heart Federation (WHF), an umbrella organization of more than 190 foundations and cardiological societies, Sania is primarily responsible for developing strategies for heart foundations on the global level. She also currently chairs the committee on the globally observed World Heart Day initiative, a major advocacy and public awareness campaign coordinated by WHF in collaboration with WHO and UNESCO.

Sania is a council member of the Foundation's Council Initiative for Cardiovascular Research in the Developing Countries (IC Health), based in Geneva, and a member of the executive board of the Geneva-based International Non-Governmental Coalition Against Tobacco. Her work spans six continents—from capacity building of African, Eastern European, and Asian heart foundations and networks in collaboration with major international health agencies, to advising governments, to defining the relationship between poverty and health, to developing and implementing the concept of franchising in health. She has published two books: *Coronary Heart Disease Prevention in South Asia* (Islamabad, Pakistan: SAARC Cardiac Society, 2002); and *The Integrated Framework for Action: A Concerted Approach to NCD in the Developing Countries* (2004). In addition, she has published twenty-seven papers.

Notwithstanding her awesome international credentials, Heartfile, headquartered in Islamabad, is Sania's pride and joy. It is a nonprofit foundation that emerged in a developing country focusing on health promotion and noncommunicable disease prevention and control (http://heartfile.org). Throughout our interview, she often referred to her company with enthusiasm.

During my first conversation with Sania, I was shy and felt inadequate in the presence of so accomplished a woman, for truly she is a pioneer in global health care strategies for the developing world. She smiled at me, waiting patiently for my first question, knowing, yet not acknowledging that her business manager was outside the door waiting with a list of urgent decisions and international phone calls that required her attention. I began with a "warm-up" question, by asking her what kind of world she wanted her children to be raised in. She was gently folding the brilliant emerald green shawl that cascaded down into her lap from her shoulders. Without hesitation she simply replied, "One in which they would not be judged by their color, ethnicity, and religious background." I was surprised by the immediacy of her answer and its simplicity and directness.

I continued my interview of this well-traveled woman by asking her to describe some of the changes she faced as a female physician in Pakistan. She thought for a moment and answered: "I have felt all along that women need to work twice as much and need to be twice as bright to 'compete' with men—but that is a generic issue and one that is not confined to the Pakistani context." Sania took a sip of mineral water and paused as if to organize many thoughts she was eager to verbalize. She continued: "By and large my professional experience has been positive in relation to my role as a woman and as a physician. However, my experiences are not representative of women in general within the country. The bias against women in this part of the world is well known, and its severity is, in many ways, unique. It is not acceptable for women, in many urban underprivileged areas and in the rural areas, to work and be seen out of their traditional roles."

I was surprised and pleased by her candor and by her willingness to admit that the bias against women in Pakistan and South Asia can be severe, for not all the Pakistani women I interviewed admitted this, and some even indicated they believed it to be untrue.

Intrigued by her choice to dedicate herself to improving health care for the poor in the developing world, I wanted to know more about health care for poor Pakistanis, so I asked Sania how the health situation in Pakistan could be improved, especially for women. Her reply was immediate, and in its immediacy gave the impression that the topic was never far from her thoughts. "The health status of women cannot be extricated from the overarching social sector and political environment. Fifty-seven years after the inception of Pakistan, despite heavy commitments made in building hospitals, laying down extensive—and perhaps by infrastructure standards, one of the most elaborate—primary health care infrastructures, the failure to impact desired health outcomes is a glaring reality within the country.

"Within this context, three critical health policy failings are worthy of note. These relate to the generation and utilization of evidence, the planning process, and the implementation of stipulated polices. These failings have been compounded by poor governance, lack of accountability, and structural health-systems-level issues characterized by inefficient and unsustainable financing and service delivery." I thought to myself how lucky the rural and poor women of Pakistan are to have such an articulate advocate as Sania arguing with government ministers, United Nations officials, and World Health Organization directors on their behalf, so encyclopedic is her knowledge and so persuasive her reasoning.

Curious, I pursued the topic, asking, "How can Pakistani health care be reformed to achieve these goals?" Again her reply was immediate, as if these thoughts were all lined up in her mind, waiting for her lips to publish to the world: "Many of these issues are interlinked with overall economic and social development and hence amenable to long-term remedial processes. Many others, however, need to be addressed as part of the health-sector reform process. Targeted capacity development, evidence-based planning, improved governance and accountability must be a hallmark of such an effort. In addition there is a need to develop new mechanisms for improving health outcomes amongst the most vulnerable and a need to go beyond the public health system and catalyzing extra action through community and private channels. It is quite evident that without such structural and concerted reform measures across a range of issues affecting the health sector, Pakistan's commitment to improve the health status of women cannot be met."

I wanted to know more about how being a Muslim woman impacted her chosen work, so I continued with the interview, asking, "Being a Muslim woman, do you face any challenges in modern Pakistani society?" Her answer surprised me. "No, actually, I do not personally face any challenges. But mine is an unusual situation as I have a supportive family and a husband that encourages me to make full use of whatever talent and skill I have. I also have a very supportive mother-in-law who looks after my children when I am frequently overseas and takes charge of the house when I am away. However, this is not the usual story within the country. Husbands are, by and large, not supportive at all of their wives' professional pursuits, especially if they entail heavy demands on their time. The closely knit family structure is usually not supportive of daughters-in-law engaging in activities other than housewifely duties. Outside of their homes, women—especially underprivileged women—are subject to undue harassment, and our poor judicial system is unable to give them protection. Therefore, except in unusual circumstances in the higher socioeconomic class, there are significant impediments to a woman's progressive role in the society."

I wanted to know more about Sania's struggle to balance being a Muslim and being a physician in Pakistan, so I asked her to explain her top three priorities as a Muslim woman physician in Pakistan. She seemed to warm to me then, pausing and moving into a more comfortable position on the sofa, and smiling at me as the setting sun washed glowing deep reds and golden oranges across the room where we sat. She replied: "Most religions preach the same values centered on peace, love, forgiveness and harmony. Though it is not my mandate to focus on such overarching priorities, I do nevertheless feel strongly, as an inhabitant of this planet, that my foremost priority is to contribute to such outcomes at a global level, in whatever little way that I can. My second priority is to contribute to fostering an orientation on 'outcomes,' on 'priority' initiatives within the ambit of social service delivery at a global level. And perhaps my third is to be able to reach out to the disadvantaged and to use my ability to alleviate suffering." I marveled at her answer: What an altruistic soul she is!

Given that Sania is one of the most widely traveled persons I have ever met, I asked: "As president of Heartfile, you travel often between Pakistan, South Asia, Europe, and the United States. How do you characterize the major differences between Muslim women in Pakistan and women in the Western world?"

She thought for a moment and then answered: "The state of women is largely heterogeneous within cultures across the globe. Notwithstanding, women in Pakistan, as indeed in any other countries, suffer many biases. However, the severity of such biases is unique in South Asia—you may have heard of honor killings—but in recent years significant attempts are being made to address some of these issues. Though I come purely from a private sector base, I must laud the efforts of our present government for the proactive role that they have taken in order to improve the lives of women in this country."

I wondered what kind of a family could produce such an accomplished and polished woman, but as I sat forward to ask my next question, her business manager politely knocked and entered the room to remind her about some important appointments she needed to keep. Sania remained polite and gracious with me, and encouraged me to continue our interview, which she appeared to be enjoying as much as I. So I introduced my next question: "Is being a Muslim woman in the modern world different from the experiences of your mother's or grandmother's generation in Pakistan?" She looked out the window and smiled as if looking back across years, remembering her family fondly before softly replying, "Yes, it is actually—there is increased acceptability of women in professional careers and public life now." She said no more, yet I somehow knew her mind was full of thoughts and sweet memories. Although I was intrigued, it was not my place to intrude upon such personal memories, nor did my limited time with her allow such luxury.

I wanted to ask one more question, to enjoy a few more

minutes in Sania's charming and enlightening company, so I asked what she, as a Pakistani Muslim woman, would tell the people of the United States if she could tell them anything. She paused for a moment and then very softly answered: "I would tell them that all religions teach the same values—love, peace, forgiveness, justice, solidarity, and equity in relationships. There is a very fine line between our respective beliefs, and we must try not to capitalize on the differences but seek common grounds for peaceful and mutually reinforcing coexistence."

The simplicity of Sania's answer was profound, and I sat quietly for a while, absorbing all her answers in the quickly darkening room. I wanted to ask her more questions, to probe more deeply into the life of a woman doctor in Pakistan, to eagerly seek answers to the numerous questions that stemmed from her comments, but I knew I must relinquish this remarkable and inspiring woman back to the developing world and back to the Pakistanis who direly needed her energy, her enthusiasm, and her expertise. I knew that my new friend was being called back to her busy life serving the women and the poor of Pakistan who suffered in silence from chronic diseases, with precious few to speak for them. How fortunate they are to have a woman such as Dr. Sania Nishtar to care so completely, unselfishly, and passionately for them.

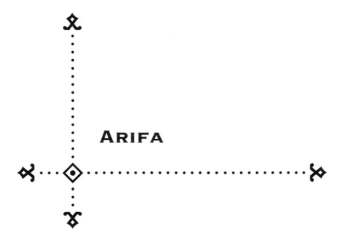

# ARIFA

ARIFA is a beautiful, petite woman with shoulder-length jet black hair, dark expressive eyes, and soft, radiant skin. She was somewhat shy at first, but opened up when we discovered a common love: books. As we chatted, Arifa stressed her lifelong love of reading. She explained that although her favorite books were fiction, she had recently become particularly interested in learning about different cultures around the world. This, in turn, had inspired her to travel.

Arifa was born in Lahore, Pakistan, and started her education at a small school near her home. When she was in her second class, Arifa's father was transferred to Peshawar, and the family moved there for two years before returning to Lahore.

After finishing Class 5, Arifa was admitted to an army school and completed her secondary education. She then graduated from Lahore College, a renowned college in Pakistan, and obtained a master's degree in statistics from Punjab University, another prestigious Pakistani university. Afterward, she taught math in a high school for four years. Arifa explained that she had learned many lessons about working with different kinds of people from teaching in a high school and said that she enjoyed the job thoroughly. When we spoke, she was not employed outside the home and was happily awaiting the birth of her first child.

I started my interview with Arifa by asking if being a Muslim woman in the modern world was in any way different from the experiences of her mother's or grandmother's generation in Pakistan. "Oh, indeed!" she enthused. "There are differences not only in the Western world, but also in Pakistan. My grandmother's time was quite different. The women did not have as much freedom of thought as we have these days. Islam gave and still gives a lot of rights to women, but sometimes Muslim women find it difficult to properly make use of those rights. As far as my experience in the modern world, it has been a good one."

When I asked Arifa what she, as a Pakistani Muslim woman, would tell the people of the United States if she could tell them anything, she replied: "I would love to tell them the value of the family system which we hold so dear in Pakistan. The respect and love which we receive and give being grandmothers, mothers, sisters, and wives is miraculous. The protection which we receive from our male siblings and family members is comforting. The people of the United States may feel as though we do not receive proper rights and that our system is one in which there is no equal opportunities for women. However, it is a great relief that the responsibility of the household income is fulfilled by the male siblings."

In addition, Arifa stated that she would like her children to be raised in a peaceful world where there is protection, freedom, and the opportunity for her children to live their lives according to their wishes.

When I asked what it meant to her to be both a Muslim and a woman, she responded: "Being a Muslim is one of the best things that ever happened to me, and I love being a woman, too. Being a Muslim woman, I believe I have my own identity. You may have noticed that all the women you see around you every day, on the streets or in shops, are women of other races, countries, and beliefs, but a Muslim woman stands out because she always has a separate identity through her appearance."

I was curious whether Arifa found that anything besides appearances made her different from other women, so I asked her if, as a Muslim woman, she saw any differences between herself and women of other religions. She replied, "I simply feel more protected."

To expand upon that thought, I asked her how she thought

Americans in particular viewed Muslim women and whether she felt misunderstood in any way. She responded, "I have not faced any problems."

In addition, I asked Arifa if she saw any reason why Americans and Muslim women could not get along well. She replied thoughtfully: "I don't think that there should be any problems. Islam is a religion that teaches respect towards other people no matter what their religion is. From what I have seen, Americans seem to be quite open-minded people who respect the independence and rights of others. I have some American friends, and they are quite nice people. We respect one another's religious feelings, and greet one another on religious occasions."

I wondered if there were any changes she would like to see in Pakistani society toward Muslim women in terms of social reform or jobs. She replied, "Pakistani society is already making progress in these regards, but if more opportunities are provided in terms of female education, there will be some very good effects."

Next, I requested that Arifa list her top three priorities in life. She answered without hesitation: "To be a good Muslim, to live with my husband and children happily in a protected environment, and to be able to do something for my country in the field of education."

Finally, I asked her if the events of September 11, 2001, had changed the way she viewed Islam, the Western world, or the interaction between Pakistan and the Western world. Arifa responded: "My views of Islam have not changed: They are the same as they were before September 11. Islam is a religion of peace. Islam respects other religions and forbids terrorism."

I continued with this line of inquiry, asking whether her views of the Western world had changed since the events of September 11. She thought a minute before replying: "As for my views on the Western world, although they have not really been changed, my views toward Western leaders have changed. Western leaders just want to take actions that benefit themselves. They vow to fight against terrorism, so they attack Afghanistan and Iraq, while at the same time they are happy to close their eyes to the injustices taking place in Palestine. They kill innocent women, children, and elders and call it a 'fight against terrorism.' That is definitely not okay."

Arifa's comments were revealing in many respects. A strong and bold woman, she was not afraid to point out injustices that she found evident in both Eastern and Western countries. At the same time, she encouraged respect and tolerance between the two parts of the world. She touted the benefits of family institutions and bonds in Pakistan and urged people around the world to look on different cultures with an open mind and heart.

# PHOTO GALLERY

A MUSLIM WOMAN *walks alone down a street in Rawalpindi to collect her children from school. She has no fear walking alone in any part of town because the Koran admonishes everyone to respect women, making it unthinkable for her to be attacked or robbed on the street. However, many women do not go out of the house alone because some neighbors consider this an immodesty; also, those families who always chaperone their women are admired and believed to have a good, strong, and honorable family life.*

**A WOMAN** *cleans the entrance to her mosque in Lahore. She was born in this neighborhood and will almost certainly die in or near the house in which she was born. She is barefoot and does this work daily, except on Friday, the Muslim holy day, when she will attend mosque at midday and then relax with friends and family at a leisurely afternoon meal. That special meal might include a small portion of meat, a luxury item. She knows everyone in the neighborhood, grew up with them, and she will grow old with them. Muslims call one another "brother" and "sister," and ties among neighbors are extremely close and dear by Western standards. She is proud of her humble place in society. As I watched her work all morning long in the hot sun, there was no end to the stream of neighbors who stopped her to chat, spread news, or idle gossip, or offered a little humor or kind remark. By Western standards she is poor, but in her neighborhood she is respected, useful, and happy.*

OBSERVING "EYE PURDAH" by modestly averting her gaze downward while in the presence of a man, a woman stands in front of her home in the village of Chiniot. Note the superb workmanship of the intricately carved turquoise wooden balcony. Chiniot is the most famous city in Pakistan for wood carvings and exquisite carpentry. In a region heavily forested with woods ideal for carving, such as almond, mango, and oak, and situated at the crossroads of the "silk road" trade route linking the Western subcontinent of Afghanistan and the Central Asian states to the Eastern subcontinent of India and Bangladesh, Chiniot played a major role during the Mughal Empire and became the center for wood craftsmanship of the highest standards. These fine skills were passed from generation to generation down through the centuries of Mughal rule and flourish to this day. This woman is proud of her home and the thousands of hours of human labor lavished upon its construction three generations ago, attested to by the careful architectural upkeep she has overseen.

**A TYPICAL TRUCK** *of a Pakistani long-distance driver displays vibrant colors and a gaudiness bordering on the indescribable. Proud of their profession and universally admired by Pakistanis, these drivers see all of Pakistan, a land of awesome beauty with some of the world's most diverse scenery, from the three highest mountain ranges in the world (Himalayas, Karakorams, and Hindu Kush) through the ancient Indus River Valley and fertile Punjab region, to the teeming coastal city of Karachi on the Arabian Sea. I and the Pakistani children around me simply stopped and stared, speechless, at the overdone opulence of these trucks while the drivers napped in hammocks and ate grilled kabobs in the shade of a roadside truck stop. The profession of truck driver is much envied in Pakistan, for these men are thought to be free and prosperous. Sadly, no women may enter this profession, for a woman who travels so far alone without a male escort would be perceived as bringing too great a scandal to bear upon herself and her family.*

**A Muslim woman** *chats with neighbors while washing her feet prior to entering the neighborhood mosque for Friday Sabbath prayers. Muslims always take off their shoes or sandals (if they own a pair) and wash their feet before entering a mosque. This action not only keeps the holy place clean, it symbolizes the leaving behind of the dirt and sins of one's life before entering into the holy place of Allah. In the absence of a newspaper, all the news and gossip of the day are exchanged in countless scenes such as this across the neighborhoods of Pakistan. The small intricately decorated structure sits above the tomb of Hazrat Ali Hajueri, one of the most prominent Muslim scholars of Pakistan; the entire site is a mosque.*

A MUSLIM WOMAN *walks to the butcher shop to purchase freshly butchered halal meat for the day's meal in a village in the Punjab, the bread and rice basket of Pakistan. It is typical for women to walk daily to a bakery to procure bread still warm and fragrant, a halal butcher shop (for those who can afford a small portion of daily meat), and a greengrocer for the freshest of produce, which they will cook with savory spices imparting strong aromas and full flavors. This woman will chat with many friends and neighbors as she goes about her hours of shopping. She has lived in this neighborhood all her life; most likely she was born and will die here, so these streets are an endless sea of familiar faces, and with each person she knows, good manners dictate that a kind word be exchanged.*

**THE AUTHOR** *is seated on a sofa with her parents on the right and a Pakistani woman friend on the left. In Pakistan a man must never sit on a sofa next to a woman unless he is married to her or is her father, brother, or son. For this reason the author is seated by the Pakistani woman hostess, separating the woman from the author's father.*

**THE EXQUISITE** *seventeenth-century Badshahi mosque in Lahore was built by the Mughal emperor Shah Jehan. Mosques are typically square or rectangular with a center courtyard. A tall, thin tower called a minaret is located at each corner of the courtyard. It is from these minarets, such as the one seen in the upper right corner, that imams call the faithful to prayer five times per day. In Islam, neither animal nor human may be depicted in art or architecture on or in a mosque, as this would defile the holy place of Allah. Therefore, intricate geometrical patterns adorn both the interiors and exteriors of mosques. This timeless design speaks to the superb craftsmanship and attention to detail of the artists and architects who fashioned this mosque.*

IN A SMALL VILLAGE *in North Central Paki-*
*stan, a woman carries the day's laundry on her head. She treads*
*slowly up the dirt path from the stream where she washed her*
*family's clothes using a small amount of soap and slapping the*
*wet garments on smooth rocks, worn from generations of such*
*use. She will hang these clothes to dry in the hot sun on the roof-*
*tops and from clothes lines. The men are about their agricultural*
*work in the fields. Five times per day, regardless of where family*
*members may find themselves, all will kneel toward Mecca and*
*pray, as prescribed for all Muslims worldwide. The large num-*
*ber of clothes of all sizes indicates that this family is typical in*
*including several generations in one household.*

**A WOMAN** *in a small town in the Punjab rides through crowded streets happily ensconced on the family vehicle, which is a small motor scooter. Her husband is driving and their seven-year-old son is up front. The scooter not only suffices for their needs but also testifies to some affluence. Muslim women in Pakistan are extremely close to their families, and family life is a very strong, intense experience by Western standards. Whether traveling through streets thronged with pedestrians and donkey carts, or engaged in activities with extended families so intensely personal and interactive, Pakistani Muslim women do not find life boring or seek to fill empty hours. Rather, there are not enough hours in the day for all their family-oriented and lively activities.*

**A WOMAN** smiled at me, happy to see a Western woman walk down her street. The Koran teaches that a visitor is a gift from Allah, and Pakistani Muslim women are delighted to see visitors from abroad. Many of these women are poor by Western standards, but they have enough food and clothing to live healthy, fulfilled lives, and the hospitality and generosity they offered me were stunning. As I walked down this street, an old man who repairs shoes curbside (he owns no shop nor even a stall or tent) cried out in a loud voice in Urdu: "Thank you for visiting us! A visitor is a gift from Allah!" and everyone on the street turned and smiled appreciatively at me.

THE AUTHOR *and her parents were invited into the home of a Pakistani family and treated with remarkable hospitality. This proud grandmother and grandfather play joyfully with their grandson. Pakistanis believe that people, not money or things, bring happiness to the soul. Seated at the right is the author's mother. The decorations on the wall proclaim the second birthday of the grandchild, which is a particularly important birthday in Pakistani families.*

BOYS *in a Pakistani mosque attend a madrasas—a religious school under the direction of an imam. Strictly segregated by gender, girls attend an all-girl school with female teachers, and boys attend an all-boy school with male teachers. In Islam, male and female roles are distinct and begin at birth. Pakistani Muslims see no discrimination in this regard, as they believe Allah created man and woman to complement one another in the fullness of nature and in the important mission of family life and child rearing. These boys were memorizing the Koran, and some will have the entire Koran memorized by the age of seven. The day I visited was hot and there is no air-conditioning, so learning took place in the shade under the giant eaves of the mosque. A poor boy may attend, and alms to the mosque and school will provide for his meager lunch, Koran, and bookstand. These boys will not learn other subjects such as mathematics, science, or computer skills; in fact, most have never touched a computer. Upon graduation, they will go off into the world, each unto his own station in life. The majority are poor and will labor for a living; a few lucky ones might have a chance at a technical education, but university education is rare and special in Pakistan.*

THE AUTHOR *and her parents stand in the great plaza in front of the famous Badshahi mosque in Lahore, built over a span of two centuries by different emperors. They have removed their shoes as required to enter the mosque and its large courtyard.*

THE CROWDED STREETS *of Islamabad provide an infinite collage of sights, sounds, smells, and tastes as a Muslim woman makes her daily walk to her grandmother's house. It is not unusual for each child and grandchild to visit their parents and grandparents on a daily basis, which shows respect and provides joys and comforts of seeing family each day to elders. These visits are not fifteen-minute visits: They last for one or two hours because hurrying would be insulting and would defeat the purpose of the visit. In fact, rushing through the events of the day is a Western tendency, not a Pakistani practice. In this ancient tradition of daily visits to parents and grandparents, the loneliness of old age is alleviated and the empty afternoon hours filled with joys.*

**THE AUTHOR** *laughs with Memoona. Although their ideas, experiences, and perspectives are different in many ways, a strong friendship developed.*

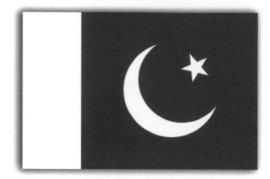

*The flag of Pakistan*

*The emblem of Pakistan*

# ISLAM:
# A BRIEF SUMMARY

**ISLAM** is an ancient monotheistic religion predominant in the Middle East. A Muslim (the word means "one who submits") is an adherent of Islam. Muslims follow the teachings of Muhammad, whom they consider to be the last and most important of the prophets sent by God. Muslims share common beliefs with Christians and Jews, whom they regard as "People of the Book." Today, there are more than one billion Muslims in the world, and the religion continues to spread. In fact, Islam is both the largest and the fastest-growing religion in the world.

Muhammad was born into the leading tribe of Mecca in 570 C.E. and was orphaned while still a young boy. He was a hardworking shepherd who, after marrying, became the successful manager of his wealthy wife's caravan. As he grew older, he would often retreat to a cave on Mount Hira to contemplate and praise God. According to Muslim teachings, on one such visit in 610 C.E., the archangel Gabriel appeared to Muhammad and told him to recite praises of God. This is known as the Night of Power and Excellence. Throughout the life of Muhammad and until his death twenty-two years later, he would receive many more messages. At once, he began to spread the messages he had received to the people of Mecca, but they were polytheists and were thus very hostile. So in 622 C.E. Muhammad migrated to Medina, a city in the North, to propagate his message. This move is known as the *Hijrah*, and it marks the date from which Muslims begin their calendar. The people of Medina were responsive to Muhammad's message, and his teachings spread until most of Arabia had converted to Islam by the time of his death in 632 C.E.

Muslims believe Muhammad is the Seal of the Prophets, meaning that he revealed the will of God truly and completely, and therefore there will be no need for God to send another prophet. Just as Christians believe that Jesus is the definitive statement of God to all humankind, Muslims believe that Muhammad is the final and definitive prophet. Although Muhammad is regarded as human, Muslims believe that he ascended into Heaven, and they revere the significance of this holy event.

CHIARA ANGELA KOVARIK

The Koran, the Muslims' holy book and the centerpiece of Islamic teachings, records recitations Muhammad was commanded to speak by the archangel Gabriel. Muhammad, who was illiterate, dictated to scribes who wrote the Koran. The second most important source of authority in Islam is the Sunnah, a book recording some of the actions and teachings of Muhammad. The worldwide community of all Muslims, referred to as the Umma, is united by the Sharia, or divine law. These teachings are taken from the Koran and the Sunnah and set forth rules and regulations on how one is to practice Islam.

Islam's central teachings are based on the Koran and the Sunnah. Muslims believe the one and only God, known as Allah, is genderless and transcendent, while at the same time personal. There are ninety-nine names for Allah, including The Real and The Compassionate, which allow Muslims to describe Allah in multiple ways. Abraham is believed to be the father of the Arab people and his son Ishmael is the ancestor of the Arabs. Abraham is thus the father of all three of the great monotheistic religions of the world: Judaism, Islam, and Christianity.

Muslims believe that the nature of humans is essentially good, but when humans forget their basic goodness, they can be led to sin by various temptations. Those who are honorable in life are rewarded in Heaven, and those who are evil are condemned to Hell. Allah judges the immortal soul of each person upon their death, granting them eternal reward or punishment.

Islam reveres the natural world because it is the creation of Allah, and is supportive of science and mathematics as a way to learn more about creation. Our world has been enriched by heights of architectural, mathematical, and artistic achievements throughout the history of Islam, including the construction of the Taj Mahal in India (the tomb of a Muslim emperor's beloved wife), the Alhambra in Spain, and the discovery of the number zero, which eluded Western mathematicians for centuries and made possible important advancements in mathematics.

Muslims follow a series of five basic practices, known as the Five Pillars of Islam: the confession of faith, prayer, fasting, wealth sharing, and pilgrimage to Mecca. The first pillar, the confession of faith, is known as the *Shahada*. It is translated as "There is no god except God, and Muhammad is God's prophet." This is a succinct statement of the beliefs that make a person a Muslim.

The second pillar is prayer. At five prescribed times a day (morning, noon, afternoon, sunset, and evening), all Muslims must prostrate themselves in the direction of Mecca and pray. In fact, many of the women I interviewed for this book interrupted our interviews to kneel on a carpet facing in the direction of Mecca to observe this Islamic requirement. The holy day for Muslims (their Sabbath) is Friday, and on Friday men must go to a mosque, the Muslim place of worship, to pray and hear a sermon given by a holy leader known as an imam.

CHIARA ANGELA KOVARIK

The third pillar of Islam, fasting, takes place during the month of Ramadan. During Ramadan Muslims abstain from eating, drinking, smoking, and sex from dawn until sunset. Even water cannot be taken during daylight hours in Ramadan, except by pregnant women. In fact, in Pakistan I watched as construction workers laboring during Ramadan in the hot sun fainted from dehydration and were carried by fellow workers to the shade under a tree. Because Muslims observing Ramadan are temporarily deprived of the material and sensual pleasures of life, they are able to achieve insight into the situations of less fortunate people. Similarly, some Christian denominations, in particular Catholics, fast during Lent, as do Jews during Yom Kippur. Self-denial is a spiritual exercise as old as Islam and Christianity, which helps the pilgrim achieve spiritual strength through discipline and the experiencing of hardship. Ramadan is determined by the Hijah (Islamic) calendar, which has twelve months, each new month beginning at sunset of the day on which the crescent moon appears. Because the Islamic calendar is lunar based, the Islamic year completes in 354 days, so Ramadan begins and ends earlier each year than the previous year. Every eleven years Ramadan cycles through the complete Western calendar of twelve months.

The fourth pillar, wealth sharing, assures that everyone in the Muslim community, the *Umma*, is economically stable. All Muslims who are economically well-off are required to give 2.5 percent of their income to a public treasury for distribution to the poor. One of the lasting memories burned upon my heart from my travels in Pakistan is the image of everyone giving alms and other forms of aid to beggars, widows, orphans, and any Muslim in need. The strength of this virtue of the Pakistanis goes far beyond what one witnesses in this regard in Europe or North or South America as practiced by Christians and other citizens of those continents. The generosity and concern demonstrated by fellow Muslims are truly awesome to behold. In Pakistan, even the poor give alms to those who are poorer than they.

The final pillar of Islam is the hajj, the pilgrimage to Mecca that all Muslims are obliged to make once in their lifetime. Pilgrims who die on the journey are revered as martyrs and assured a place in eternal Paradise. The pilgrimage involves ritual acts, such as circling the Ka'ba, a structure thought to have been built by Abraham, and wearing simple symbolic clothes. These clothes are intended to make all Muslims equal at the hajj, regardless of differences in caste, wealth, or station in life.

Time and again, the women I met who had been privileged enough to make the pilgrimage to Mecca, marveled at the feelings of equality they perceived among all Muslims during the hajj. It was as if that concrete realization of their equality before Allah and before one another had become a central point of their awareness during the very moving experience of the hajj.

Muslims believe the body belongs to God and therefore must be taken care of and never abused. Ritual washing must occur before prayer, and clothing should not be revealing. Islam regulates the diet, forbidding the eating of pork and shellfish, or animals that eat other live or dead animals (carnivores or scavengers), and the drinking of alcoholic beverages. Sexuality is considered a great gift from Allah and is forbidden outside of marriage, as are prostitution and homosexual acts. Polygamy is permitted for men, although the number of men who have one wife far exceeds the number of men who have more than one simultaneous wife. Men are allowed multiple wives, and most Muslims take this to mean that a man may have up to four simultaneous wives, but only if he is able to maintain equality among them. However, some Muslims do not believe the number of simultaneous wives is limited to four.

The veiling of women was a practice that existed in Arabia and is no longer universal among women in the Muslim community. The degree and type of veiling have different meanings in different socioeconomic and geographic spheres of Pakistan, but the wearing of the veil always stems from the need for women to maintain modesty and prevent scandal in their community.

An important personal and social aspect of Islam is the concept of *jihad*, which means "exertion" or "struggle." Jihad is sometimes called the sixth pillar of Islam, and the term refers to an individual's spiritual struggle against anything that takes away from the revering of Allah and His divine will. Sometimes, jihad is interpreted to mean "holy war," but the Koran states clearly that war is only to take place as a means of self-defense. The reader of the Koran is cautioned to explore the context of this often misunderstood or misinterpreted word.

Nations with large percentages of Muslims lie in North Africa, the Middle East, Southwestern Asia, South Asia, and Malaysia and Indonesia in Southeast Asia. Only about 20 percent of Muslims live in Arabia or are Arabs. In South Asia alone, the three nations of Pakistan, Bangladesh, and India contain about one-third of the world's Muslims. In 1947, the British redrew the map that defined these three countries, and many Muslims left what is today India to take up residence in Pakistan and Bangladesh (known at the time as West Pakistan and East Pakistan, respectively). As a result, India remains mostly Hindu, whereas Pakistan and Bangladesh are almost entirely Muslim.

There is only one version of the Koran, a fact that unites all Muslims worldwide. However, most Muslims in the world (about 85 percent) are Sunni, which is shorthand for "the Sunnah of the Prophet." This is the mainstream branch of Islam in the world today. A minority of Muslims are Shi'i, shorthand for the term "Shi'at Ali," which means "Partisans of Ali." They are divided over the issue of succession to the Prophet Muhammad. Ali was the cousin and son-in-law of the Prophet, and was passed over three times as Muhammad's successor. Eventually he was named successor (Caliph), but he was later assassinated. Ali's son Husayn also was assassinated, in 680 C.E. Today, Iran, Iraq, Kuwait, Afghanistan, and Pakistan all have large Shi'i populations: In Iran and Iraq, Shi'is constitute the majorities. Shi'is revere an Imam as a distinguished figure and leader with special spiritual gifts; Sunnis do not have such an exalted figure.

Islam is one of the world's greatest philosophical and theological accomplishments, a beautiful and profound religion steeped in scriptural tradition. Its rich and wonderful history has influenced art, music, literature, and architecture for more than twelve hundred years. Islam has spread all over the globe and today is both the largest and the fastest-growing religion in the world. Attracting believers from every walk of life because of its emphasis on the goodness of humanity, its strong sense of community, the equality of all Muslims, and the all-encompassing love of God, Islam continues to spread the message of Muhammad today as effectively as it did twelve centuries ago.

Information in this chapter is
adapted from the CIA *World
Factbook* for Pakistan.

## WOMEN AND THE
## DIVISION OF SPACE
## IN PAKISTAN

*Purdah* is the Persian word for curtain, and in
Muslim societies purdah refers to the degree of veiling a woman
observes. In a larger sense, the term refers to the separating
of women from men in daily life, both physically and sym-
bolically. There is great variety in the degree to which Muslim
women observe purdah, both globally among the world's more
than one billion Muslims, and among Muslim women in Pakistan. Rural women of the North Western Frontier Territories
(NWFT) tend to observe the strictest purdah, and educated
women of Lahore and Islamabad who have some contact with
the Western world or diplomatic corps tend to observe the
least strict form of veiling. In addition, many Muslim women

> 101

observe "eye purdah," which requires a woman to avert her gaze or lower her eyes when she interacts with men outside the family, as a sign of her modesty.

A family's honor rests on its women, and the men of the family place restrictions on female family members' freedom of movement, behavior, and activities of the women to maintain family honor. Depending on one's place in society and the region of Pakistan in which a woman lives, a woman improperly veiled or going too freely beyond the confines of the home can bring dishonor to her family, principally through neighborhood gossip. For example, a woman's prospects for marriage are seriously diminished if she is judged immodest or to have dishonored her family by excessive activity outside the house. Serious consequences can arise over issues of purdah, and a woman who moves about too freely can be considered shameless, although this is less true in the wealthier districts of large cities such as Lahore and Islamabad.

It is easy for Westerners to misunderstand the importance of this concept of family honor and how strong an influence it can be on the choices family members make. For example, suppose an older sister wishes to wear no veil, or to attend college, or in the rural areas simply to attend high school. At least at this point in her life, she might not care if her marriage opportunities are diminished by her actions; however, her choices could render her younger sisters or even her brothers undesirable for marriage in the eyes of prospective spouses and their families.

Such considerations complicate matters, and some women, even though they may personally be willing to bear these risks for themselves, might reluctantly choose to conform for the sake of their siblings' futures or their parents' respectability. Some Westerners would scoff at such viewpoints and compromises, but these matters are seen differently in Pakistan.

Many Pakistani women spend most of their lives within their homes and courtyards, and when they go out they are always accompanied by chaperones, be they other women, brothers, fathers, or other male family members.

Rural women whose labor is required on their families' farms have more freedom to be unveiled and are more mobile than urban women, by the necessity of their work. Their need to tend the animals, move about the area, and take the harvest to market requires a relaxed view of purdah. For example, they need to walk to the marketplace and haggle with men over the price of eggs or argue about the quality of their daily vegetable harvest.

The strictest purdah in Pakistan is observed in the North West Frontier Province and Balochistan. Here, honor killings can occur if a family perceives its honor to be insulted or even questioned. In this region women almost never leave their homes except to marry, and they seldom marry unrelated men. Some are not even allowed contact with male cousins on their mother's side because, in this strongly patriarchal society, such men are not considered relatives.

Relations in this region are very regimented. For example, women may converse with their father-in-law's paternal uncles and brothers-in-law, but only with formality. However, this region illustrates the extreme case and is not typical of the rest of Pakistan. The separation of women from men outside the family walls is principally enforced by neighborhood gossip, which is both more prevalent and more powerful in Pakistan than in Western societies.

When a Muslim woman is seated on a sofa, she may not sit next to a man except for her husband, father or brothers. An unmarried woman must never be left alone in the company of a man, although in the modern workplace this restriction is more relaxed.

In these ways and in many other ways, a woman's "space" is divided into a separate world within a world, apart from the "space" of men. The veil is not only a physical barrier of silk or linen, it is also a psychological curtain. Many Westerners perceive the veil as an encumbrance, an unfair burden placed upon women, but many Muslim women have told me that the veil in particular, and purdah in general, grant them a freedom in their own "space," apart from the world of men. Not all Muslim women would shed the veil if they were given the choice; they tell me that for them the veil "works." On the other hand, some women do not like the veil. This view is especially expressed by young Muslim women who are educated or who have contact with the Western world through friends, travel, business, or educational pursuits. Some of these women have modified or abandoned the veil and observe a greatly relaxed purdah. Also, Muslim nations such as Turkey, which have historically had centuries of close contact with Western civilization, have greatly adapted purdah and the use of the veil. All in all, purdah is not simply a veiling of the head and face. It is a complex and comprehensive set of rules and recommendations, mores and expectations, by which Muslim women interact with the outside world, with men, and even with other women.

Information in this chapter is from
www.pak.org, the official Pakistan
government general information Web site.

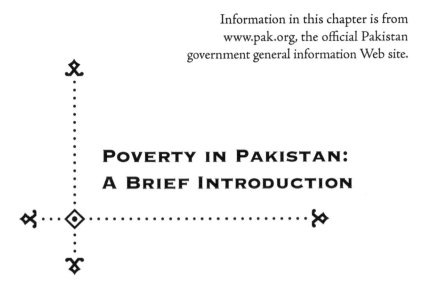

## Poverty in Pakistan:
## A Brief Introduction

IN PAKISTAN poverty has different dimensions that can be difficult to measure. The poor in Pakistan have low incomes relative to those in Western nations such as Western European countries and the United States, but figures can be misleading. With average yearly per capita earnings of US $460, Pakistanis appear abjectly poor, on paper, to Westerners. However, costs of living are much lower in South Asia than in the United States or Western Europe, so these figures can be misleading. Indeed, experts differ on a meaningful definition of poverty. Some experts focus on basic needs such as clean drinking water, basic nutrition, proper sanitation, and access to basic education and health care in defining poverty. Others focus on calories consumed per adult per day, citing 2,300 or 2,500 as a level below which poverty becomes significant because life and health are, themselves, threatened. To some extent, measures of poverty can become so abstract they become academic or manipulated by governments when basic human needs of people are not met. The very measure of poverty applied in the affluent societies of Western Europe and the United States would qualify as a middle-class lifestyle, or even better, in much of South Asia.

In my travels through Pakistan, although I met many families who were quite poor, I never met a starving or seriously malnourished person. Why? One of the Five Pillars of Islam, which is strictly observed by Muslims in Pakistan, is the giving of alms, and Pakistani Muslims feel extreme discomfort, even a type of personal agony, when they see a brother or sister Muslim in need of food, clothing, or medical care. The reader of this book will notice how many of the women I interviewed stressed that it is their duty as Muslim women to help anyone in need, some even listing this as one of their life's priorities. Although many Westerners proclaim this same noble ethic, the seriousness and intensity and daily practice are noticeably more pronounced among Muslims in South Asia than I have observed among Westerners in Europe or North America.

In 2001, the government of Pakistan established the official poverty level at 2,350 calories per adult per day, which is roughly equivalent to the amount of food which can be purchased for 750 rupees (US $15.00) per adult per month. Many people in North America or Western Europe spend this amount of money on a restaurant meal for one person. At this definition of poverty, which is much lower than any such standard used in Western Europe or the United States, about 32 percent of Pakistanis are living below the poverty line. Unlike the poor in the United States and Western Europe, these people do not have television sets, heated homes, running hot water and in some cases running water at all, or many modern conveniences. Their homes may be little more than shacks with only one or two rooms. Often, several generations live in these houses, sometimes up to four generations. Often, they do not have electricity or natural gas for heating or cooking. The people may own only one or two sets of clothes. They have no automobile and are likely illiterate.

When considering poverty in Pakistan, one must take into account the extreme youthfulness of the population, for the impact of poverty on the young is especially profound and its ramifications can be long lasting. The population of Pakistan is 160 million, but 40 percent are under the age of fifteen. The median age of the country is a mere nineteen years. This is a very young population, caused by an extremely high birthrate. Children are considered a splendid gift from Allah, the source of joy in a couple's life. In addition, Pakistanis are much less enamored of physical possessions and wealth than of large, close, and happy families. Also, children are viewed as the source of support for aging parents and grandparents, a more ancient social security system than that employed in the Western nations. The population growth rate is 2 percent, and the birthrate is more than 31 per 1,000 population. At these rates, Pakistan, which is today one of the ten most populous countries on earth, is destined to move higher on the list of the world's poorest countries. This places great stress on the poverty rating of the nation, since gains in gross domestic product must be distributed, fairly or unfairly, to increasingly more children.

The infant mortality rate is high: 75 deaths per 1,000 live births in 2004. Per woman, 4.3 children are born. Very few people have HIV/AIDS: 78,000 in 2004, both because of limited contact with foreigners and because of Islam's strict prohibitions on adultery, fornication, homosexual relations, and recreational drug use. In 2001, there were only 4,500 AIDS deaths.

The high illiteracy rate compounds the poverty problem. Among those age fifteen and over, 54 percent of the population is illiterate. Amazingly, the literacy spread between males and females is shockingly high: 41 percent of males are illiterate, and 69 percent of females are illiterate.

According to the CIA *World Factbook*, Pakistan is an impoverished and underdeveloped country, having suffered from decades of internal political disputes, low levels of foreign investment, and a costly, ongoing confrontation with neighboring India. However, the International Monetary Fund and foreign assistance, and the opening of global markets, are helping to raise Pakistan out of poverty, albeit slowly. About 8 percent of Pakistanis (one out of twelve) are unemployed.

In summary, although Pakistan is an impoverished and underdeveloped country, its future looks bright and progress against poverty is being made, in particular as the result of the world's recent trend to more open global markets. More important, few are starving in Pakistan and everyone has at least subsistence level of food and clothing due to the feeling of brotherhood and sisterhood among Pakistani Muslims and the seriousness to which the daily giving of alms to the poor is observed as one of the Five Pillars of Islam.

Information in this chapter is
adapted from the Library of Congress
Country Studies on Pakistan.

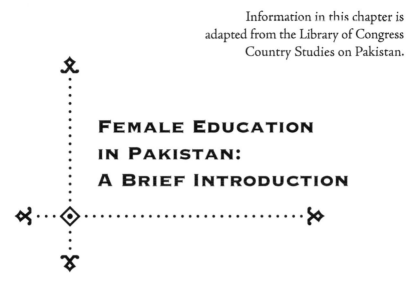

# FEMALE EDUCATION IN PAKISTAN: A BRIEF INTRODUCTION

**PAKISTANI WOMEN** suffer from a low literacy rate. There is a significant gap between women and men in the likelihood that they know how to read and write, which in Western societies is considered a fundamental right and a building block for democracy.

Recent years, however, have seen an improvement in the rate of women's literacy. In the 1980s, among women aged fifteen to twenty-four, only one-fourth of all women were literate. In 1990, the United Nations reported that for every 100 girls of primary school age, only 30 were in school, and for every 100 girls of secondary school age, only 13 were in school. Higher education is not widely available in Pakistan: the Pakistani

National Education Council of 1990 reported that 3 percent of men and 2 percent of women between the ages of seventeen and twenty-one were enrolled in degree programs.

Looking at the entire population over the age of twenty-five in Pakistan, women averaged 0.7 years of school compared with an average of 2.9 years of schooling for men.

These vast differences in education mask an even greater gap in rural areas. In 1981, only 7 percent of rural women were literate, compared with 35 percent of urban women. This contrasts with a literacy rate of 27 percent for rural men and 57 percent for urban men. Even though Pakistan is not one of the poorest countries of the world, these very low literacy rates for women are in line with those of the world's poorest countries.

Why would this be so?

The answer must go beyond the issue of money. In the 1980s, the Pakistani Ministry for Women's Development reported that a major impediment to literacy and education for young women was the perceived danger to the woman's honor and the honor of the family. Many parents fear their daughters will not be considered suitable for marriage if they are literate or educated, particularly if their prospective husbands are not literate or have limited education.

Information in this chapter is
adapted from the Library of Congress
Country Studies on Pakistan.

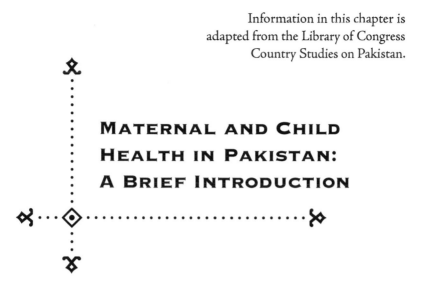

# MATERNAL AND CHILD HEALTH IN PAKISTAN: A BRIEF INTRODUCTION

IN THE 1980s, the average age of marriage for a Pakistani woman was 19.8 years. About 12 percent of women used contraception; thus many women had their first child about one year after marriage. Nationwide, about half of Pakistani women have had their first child by the age of twenty-one.

In 1990, about 30 percent of pregnant women received no prenatal medical care, and about the same percentage gave birth at home with only family or a neighborhood midwife to treat them. Among women between the ages of fifteen and forty-five, a significant percentage of deaths involve childbirth.

In a major health study spanning 1975 to 1990, about 57

percent of pregnant women were anemic, and many had vitamin deficiencies. In 1992, one out of ten infants died during their first year of life.

The good news is that progress is being made in improving maternal and child health care in Pakistan. Between 1960 and 1992, the infant mortality rate dropped from 163 per 1,000 live births, to 99 per 1,000 live births. In part this is due to a network of immunization clinics which offer free immunizations. By 1992, 81 percent of infants had received their recommended immunizations.

The situation is improving, but Pakistan is a poor nation and there are many obstacles to bringing adequate nutrition and basic modern health care to all Pakistanis, especially rural women and children.

# THE FLAG AND EMBLEM OF PAKISTAN

**THE PAKISTANI FLAG** was designed by Quaid-i-Azam Muhammad Ali Jinnah, the founder of Pakistan.

The white bar and dark green field represent minorities and the Muslim majority, respectively. The crescent represents progress; the five-pointed star symbolizes light and knowledge.

The crescent and star at the top of the emblem is a traditional symbol of Islam.

The emblem of Pakistan conveys Pakistan's ideological foundation, its cultural heritage, the guiding principles, and the agricultural basis of its economic strength. The four sections of the shield depict cotton, wheat, tea, and jute, the nation's main crops. The wreath surrounding the shield is a reproduction of the floral designs used in traditional Mughal art. The scroll supporting the shield carries the Urdu version of Jinnah's famous motto: "Faith, Unity, Discipline."

*Please see the last page of the color photo section for illustrations of the flag and emblem of Pakistan.*

# AFTERWORD

THROUGHOUT the long process of writing this book, I as the interviewer, and these brave Pakistani Muslim women as the interviewees, were changed by the very process of the interview itself. As I came to understand more fully their unique Muslim and female view of the world, so too did they come to understand me by my very questions and comments, my attentiveness to certain details, and my surprise or indifference to certain other details. They came to understand how my views as a young American woman differ from their views as Pakistani Muslim women.

I found through these interviews that when we make the effort to lift the veil, to understand Pakistani culture, and to embrace the outward differences of these women and all people worldwide, we learn that they are not so different from us. Their hopes, their dreams, and their thoughts are so similar to my own that, at times, I felt as though I was seeing and hearing reflections of myself. They love their family, their life, their religion, and their world. They yearn for peace among nations, education for their children and grandchildren, and lifelong bonds with family. They are deeply saddened by real or perceived Western mistrust or fear of their ethnicity, Muslim culture, and dress. Who among us has never felt these same emotions? Essentially, we are all the same: although we are separated by two continents and a vast ocean, and placed on opposite ends of a spectrum throughout history, the similarities between us are striking.

This realization led me to wonder whether understanding was the only true path to peace. For if we truly understand the essence of another person, we see in ourselves reflections of the same humanity that unites us all with the strongest bond imaginable. We are inextricably tied to one another with a link that transcends all the artificial or arbitrary divisions put in place by diverse cultures since the dawn of time. We all dream, love, hope, hate, and fear as genuinely as we breathe.

However, so often in our frantic, busy lives we Americans race to accomplish some goal, not grasping that in the very process of hurrying toward a goal, we ruin our hope of achieving anything of lasting worth. In our frenzied, materialistic Western culture, have we forgotten how to live, how to enjoy life's simple, sweet pleasures? When did we lose sight of the notion that knowledge is meant to be obtained, love to be spread, and understanding to be cultivated? The intimacies of life bind and connect all Pakistanis, something that is too often overlooked in Western society. To Pakistanis, life is about connecting with one another, sitting for hours with friends in a café sipping foamy, pink Pakistani tea, or visiting an elderly relative every afternoon without fail. I observed throughout the cities and villages I visited that Pakistanis took daily joys from families and neighbors, not from material possessions or career climbing. They take time each day to listen to, to learn from, and to love those around them. In my travels in Pakistan I learned that when we take the time to truly get to know and love someone, not as a "Muslim," "Christian," "Jew," "man," "woman," "American," or "Pakistani," but as a person, we accomplish the unspoken goal of humanity: peace.

This book represents a journey. When I began my journey, I had no goal but to seek knowledge—knowledge of the women around me, the world I live in, and how we all relate. Now, at my journey's end, I hope to share the knowledge I gained from my travels. Along the way, somewhere between the crowded street markets of Lahore, the chaotic traffic jams of Rawalpindi, and the quiet sitting rooms covered with handwoven silk carpets, I was changed. For many hours I was blessed with the privilege of listening to these Pakistani Muslim women tell the stories of their lives, their hopes, and their dreams. I now realize the importance of diversity in our world and the importance of accepting the rich differences between our Eastern and Western civilizations. I recognize the extent to which our place in this world community depends upon others, however distant they may be. These conclusions have shocked, confused, enlightened, and altered me.

When we complete our travels, we arrive back at the same place where we began, but we are different in fundamental ways. We as travelers have glimpsed a way of life that is poles apart from what we have known.

And so I hope that you, my readers, have also changed simply by journeying with me. As you have walked with me down the noisy, teeming streets and alleyways of Pakistan's ancient cities and rural villages, as you have drunk deep of Pakistan's Islamic culture, you have allowed these women to open for you the doors of their courtyards and of their hearts. The gift to us from these women is that we may learn to see in new ways their culture, and to understand their lives, their hopes, and their dreams. By accepting their gift, we may come to see our own culture, our own religions, and even ourselves as we have never seen them before. May we all be enriched by their generosity.

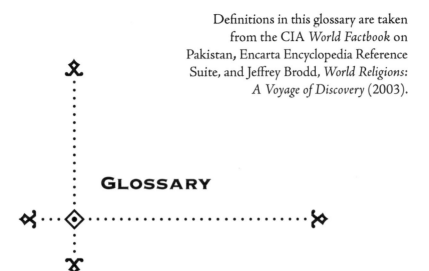

Definitions in this glossary are taken from the CIA *World Factbook* on Pakistan, Encarta Encyclopedia Reference Suite, and Jeffrey Brodd, *World Religions: A Voyage of Discovery* (2003).

## GLOSSARY

| | |
|---|---|
| *Abaya* | A black head-to-toe cloak. |
| *Allah* | The Islamic term for God (literally, "The God"). |
| *Burqa* | Fitted full-body veil worn by Muslim women for modesty. |
| *Caliphs* | Muslim leaders chosen by the community after the death of Muhammad in 632 C.E. The first caliph was Muhammad's father-in-law, Abu Bakr. |
| *Chador* | Loosely draped cloth used as a head covering and body veil. |
| *Dervish* | Initiates of Sufi orders (see definition of Sufism |

below). They are taught mystical Islamic philosophy and that Love is a projection of the essence of God to the universe; dervishes are known for whirling in trancelike meditation.

*Eye purdah*  Averting the gaze and lowering eyes to the floor when Muslim women must mix and interact with men.

*Fiqh*  Islamic jurisprudence, which is divided into two parts: The study of sources and methodology (*usul al-fiqh*: roots of the law), and the practical rules (*furu' al-fiqh*: branches of the law).

*Hajj*  The primary pilgrimage of life, required of all Muslims worldwide as one of the Five Pillars of Islam, to the Great Mosque in Mecca, where several ritual acts are performed, including washing and circling the Ka'ba, a stone structure in the courtyard.

*Halal*  The word means "permissible." Meat that is halal has been slaughtered according to the guidelines of Islamic law so as to cause the animal minimal suffering.

*Havelis*  Multistory dwellings constructed to accommodate large extended families.

*Hijaab*  A head scarf worn by Muslim women for modesty. This can vary greatly in style, fashion, and in degree of covering, in different geographic or socioeconomic strata of Pakistan.

**Hijah (Hijrah; Hijri)**  The Islamic calendar, which is based on the moon (as opposed to the Gregorian or Western calendar, which is based on the fixed seasons). This calendar has twelve months with each new month beginning at sunset on the day the crescent moon appears. Because it is based on lunar motion, the twelve months of the year constitute 354 days; therefore the months move backward through the seasons and occur approximately eleven days earlier every year.

**Hijra**  Muhammad's migration northward from Mecca to the city of Medina in 622 C.E., fleeing from hostility toward his teachings on social and economic justice. Muslims base their system of dating years on this event using the abbreviation A.H. (after *Hijra*, literally, "emigration").

**Imam**  A holy Muslim man who is believed to have special spiritual insight and is regarded as an authority.

**Jihad**  A principle of exertion or struggle which applies to all aspects of Islamic life (literally, "struggle"). This term sometimes can, but need not, refer

|  |  |
|---|---|
|  | to an armed struggle in a "Holy War for Islam" (Islamic Jihad). |
| *Ka'ba* | The stone cubical structure in the courtyard of the Great Mosque of Mecca, believed to be built by Abraham, and considered by Muslims as the "navel" (sacred geographic center) of the world. |
| *Koran (Qur'an; Quran)* | The primary sacred text of Islam; also considered to be Islam's earthly center (the word Qur'an means "recitation"). The Koran's subtle meanings conveyed in Arabic script and its inherently poetic nature render its full meaning impossible to translate into any other language. |
| *Masala* | Garam masala: a generic term similar to "curry powder" that refers to an aromatic mixture of herbs and spices that is ground fresh daily and used in family cooking. Recipes vary by region and by dish. The mixture may include cumin, fennel, coriander, cinnamon, cloves, poppy seeds, saffron, chilies, black cumin seeds, fenugreek, turmeric, raw cardamom seeds, cloves, and black pepper. |
| *Mongol* | A member of any of the traditionally nomadic peoples of Mongolia; of or relating to the region of Mongolia or its people or their languages or |

cultures. The Mongols created the most geographically vast empire in the history of the world under Genghis Khan, and swept down from Mongolia to conquer what is today Pakistan, India, and Bangladesh.

*Mughal*    One of the greatest and most extensive empires in the medieval world, a dynasty ruled by a line of Muslim emperors who reigned in India and South Asia from 1526 to 1858. The first Mughal emperor was Babur, a descendant of the Turkish conqueror Timur on his father's side and the conqueror Genghis Khan on his mother's side. Shah Jehan was another great Mughal emperor.

*Muhammad*    The founder of Islam and prophet, born in 570 C.E.

*Muslim*    A follower of Islam (literally, "one who submits").

*PBUH*    "Peace Be Unto Him"; said of the deceased, especially of the Prophet Muhammad (the equivalent of the English "Rest in peace" or the Latin "Requiescat in pacem").

*People of the Book*    Jews and Christians, who are viewed in a favored way by Muslims as having some expressions of the Divine Truth of God as revealed in their sacred texts, the Torah, Old and New Testaments. Muslims feel a certain affinity to Jews and Christians because they also share the same prophets (Muslims believe Jesus was a great prophet, but not divine), although Muslims believe the Koran is the final, definitive word of God to humankind.

*Polygamy*    The legally permitted state of a man having multiple simultaneous living wives, permitted to Muslims by the Koran, and exemplified by Muhammad in his life. Some Muslims hold that a man may have four living wives; others maintain that there is no limit. Islam requires the husband to treat all his wives equally.

*Punjab*    A fertile region of central Pakistan known as the bread and rice basket of the country for its agricultural capacity to feed the nation.

*Purdah*    The veiling of a woman, or in a larger sense the physical and symbolic separation of activities and restriction of contact between men and women (literally "curtain" in Persian).

*Ramadan*    The ninth lunar month of the Islamic calendar during which Muslims fast, as prescribed by the third of the Five Pillars of Islam.

| | |
|---|---|
| *Shahada* | The confession of faith, the first of the Five Pillars of Islam, the recitation of which makes one a Muslim: "There is no god except God, and Muhammad is God's prophet." |
| *Shalwar kameez* | The traditional clothing of Pakistan and parts of South Asia, which includes ankle-length, loose-fitting, long-sleeved robes for men, and flowing ankle-length robes for women, also long-sleeved, with head scarves, affording comfort, coolness in summer, and modesty always. |
| *Sharia* | Divine law drawn from the Koran together with the Sunnah, which specifies five categories of behavior for all Muslims: obligatory, recommended, indifferent, disapproved, and forbidden. Islam classically drew no boundary between mosque ("church") and state. |
| *Shaykh* | A teacher or master in Islam in Sufi Islam; the term can also refer to a political leader or learned religious leader, or even simply to a male elder. |
| *Shi'ism (Shi'i Islam)* | The division of Islam practiced by a minority of Muslims in the world (12 percent), dominant in Iraq and Iran, arising from a leadership dispute in the early centuries of Islam. This division differs from Sunni Islam in its hopes for a messiah, and its Imam. |

| | |
|---|---|
| *Sufi* | A follower of Sufism, the mystical form of Islam. |
| *Sufism* | The mystical form of Islam, which emphasizes the transcendent nature of God as beyond human understanding: This form draws followers from both Sunni Islam and Shi'i Islam, and therefore is not per se a division of Islam. (The word comes from *suf*, referring to the coarse woolen garment worn by Sufis.) |
| *Sunnah* | The record of the actions and teachings of Muhammad; which are carefully distinguished from the Koran (literally, "custom of the Prophet"). |
| *Sunnism (Sunni Islam)* | The division of Islam practiced by the majority of Muslims in the world (88 percent), named after the Sunnah. |
| *Surahs* | Chapters of the Koran, numbering 114. |
| *Umma* | The entire community of Muslims throughout the world (all of whom bear some responsibility for the well-being of one another). Umma transcends race, ethnicity, and nationality, language, and all cultural dimensions. |

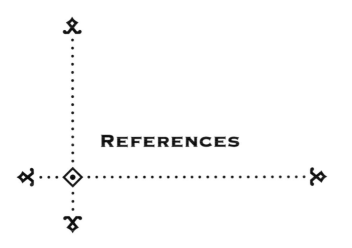

# REFERENCES

Amin, Mohamid, Duncan Willetts, and Graham Hancock. *Journey through Pakistan*. Karachi, Pakistan: Paramount Books, 1997.

Brodd, Jeffrey. *World Religions: A Voyage of Discovery*. Winona, MN: St. Mary's Press, 2003.

CIA *World Factbook* on Pakistan: http://www.odci.gov/cia/publications/factbook/geos/pk.html

Encarta Encyclopedia Reference Suite, Microsoft, Inc.

Library of Congress Country Studies on Pakistan: http://lcweb2.loc.gov/frd/cs/pktoc.html

Pakistan government general information Web site: http://www.pak.org/

To order additional copies of *Interviews with Muslim Women of Pakistan*:

Web:     www.itascabooks.com

Phone:   1-800-901-3480

Fax:     Copy and fill out the form below with credit card information.
         Fax to 763-398-0198.

Mail:    Copy and fill out the form below. Mail with check or credit card information to:

         Syren Book Company
         5120 Cedar Lake Road
         Minneapolis, MN 55416

Order Form

| Copies | Title / Author | Price | Totals |
|--------|----------------|-------|--------|
|        | *Interviews with Muslim Women of Pakistan* / **Chiara Angela Kovarik** | $14.95 | $ |
| | Subtotal | | $ |
| | 7% sales tax (MN only) | | $ |
| | Shipping and handling, first copy | | $        4.00 |
| | Shipping and handling, ____ add'l copies @$1.00 ea. | | $ |
| | TOTAL TO REMIT | | $ |

Payment Information:

| __ Check Enclosed   __ Visa/MasterCard | | |
|---|---|---|
| Card number: | Expiration date: | |
| Name on card: | | |
| Billing address: | | |
| | | |
| City: | State: | Zip: |
| Signature : | Date: | |

Shipping Information:

| __ Same as billing address   __ Other (enter below) | | |
|---|---|---|
| Name: | | |
| Address: | | |
| | | |
| City: | State: | Zip: |

00347 4825